Wolf and Dessauer

Wolf and Dessauer

WHERE FORT WAYNE SHOPPED

Jim & Kathie Barron

THE
History
PRESS

Published by The History Press
Charleston, SC 29403
www.historypress.net

Copyright © 2011 by Jim and Kathie Barron
All rights reserved

First published 2011

ISBN 978-1-5402-3049-2

Library of Congress CIP data applied for.

To our grandchildren: Isabelle, Jesse, Christine and Liam.
You are our inspiration and our joy.

CONTENTS

ACKNOWLEDGEMENTS

Years ago, before Kathie and I had ever written a book (and many more years before I had even met my future wife), I would skim over the acknowledgements pages of any particular book I happened to be reading. I was of the opinion that the acknowledgement portion of the book was only there because, well, every book had to have them, right? It makes the book look professional, and the legal department makes you put them in so it can justify the importance of its existence to the publisher.

Now, it's all too clear to me that no one writes a book all on his or her own. Especially not one like this. Thousands of people contributed to this creation, and they all deserve to be recognized, beginning with Sam Wolf and Myron Dessauer and ending with the person reading this—namely you!

It's a little like the Wolf and Dessauer Department Store itself. It took an idea started by a couple of entrepreneurs, an investment team, a group of managers, a sales force, employees, customers and, perhaps most importantly, the wide-eyed wonder of all of the children who ever looked through those magical Christmas windows. All of those people contributed to making W&D what it was, and they have, in one way or another, helped to make the book a reality.

Now comes the task of distilling all of the names down to a realistic number that can be included without becoming a separate book of its own. It's also now that we go through the process of selecting who to mention by name. It's an agonizing thing because it's inevitable that we're going to forget to mention someone who should be thanked, and we probably will remember who we missed about the time this rolls off the printing press.

ACKNOWLEDGEMENTS

We start by acknowledging family friend Donna McEvoy, who got the ball rolling the day she told our daughter, Erika, about the incredible Wolf and Dessauer window displays of bygone years. We also thank Dick and Dee Stoner and the late Bob Sievers for sharing their memories with us.

We acknowledge the late Bud and Bill Latz and the late Phil Steigerwald and his family for contributing so many recollections. We appreciate the past contributions of the Fort Wayne History Center for opening its archives to us, and we also thank the Vera Bradley Company for its past participation and its unceasing commitment to the people of Fort Wayne. Thanks as well to Melissa Cordial Schenkel and Michael Nelaboriage at Vera Bradley, who did such a wonderful job editing our original volume two.

Thank you to Claudia Shoup for her insight and encouragement in the creation of our previous W&D books. Thanks also go out to those members of the Fort Wayne media who spread the word about our first and subsequent books, thereby providing an income for our family at a time when we were destitute (that could be a book in itself).

Thanks to PBS-TV39 Fort Wayne. Thanks to Frank Gray and Nancy Venderly and all of the folks at the *Fort Wayne Journal Gazette*. Thanks to Kevin Kilbane and all of the other journalists at the *Fort Wayne News Sentinel*.

Our thanks also go to Charly Butcher of WOWO radio 1190AM for his extensive live interviews. We appreciate the people at the *Fort Wayne Reader*, *Whatzup* magazine and *Fort Wayne Business Weekly* magazine for their coverage.

We also can't forget the kindness of Eric Olsen and the news team at WPTA TV, as well as our friends at WANE TV and WISE TV for their feature stories.

Many, many thanks go out to Sue Hackleman and Chris Shatto for providing pictures and to Eric Lucas for putting us in touch with his father, Ken Lucas, who generously shared his collection of W&D photos and slides for this book.

And we can't forget the kindness of two people who, at the time, were total strangers when I walked into their shop asking if they would be interested in stocking a couple of our original Wolf and Dessauer books on their shelves. They told me to bring in as many as I wanted and became dear friends of ours in the process. So thanks to Fred, Janelle and Marti of Nature's Corner Antiques in Fort Wayne.

Thanks also to all of my co-workers at WBCL Radio for being a constant source of encouragement. Most of all, we give our thanks to our Lord Jesus Christ, who makes everything possible.

INTRODUCTION

My husband grew up on a small farm outside of Hamilton, Indiana. Trips to Fort Wayne were occasional, and Wolf and Dessauer was usually only on the list of destinations if there was time left after what was usually a lengthy excursion through every corner of Stoner's magic shop—then the men acquiesced to my mother-in-law's request to visit W&D's basement. Jim never saw the famous W&D Christmas windows or sat on Santa's lap. His only memory associated with W&D and Christmastime is watching the television show at home after school with his brothers. I have no memories of W&D at all.

I moved to Indiana from Upstate New York, but my early years were spent on Long Island just an hour's ride on the Long Island Expressway from New York City. You've probably heard people say that most New Yorkers haven't even been to the Statue of Liberty. Sadly, it's true. And so it was with this New Yorker. My family had taken me to the circus at Madison Square Garden, to the Museum of Natural History and even to the Empire State Building, but it took an old yellow school bus and a sixth-grade trip for an eleven-year-old girl to really understand what I had been missing in regard to Christmas.

I will never forget that day. There I was, standing in Rockefeller Center, dwarfed by the biggest Christmas tree in the world (or so it seemed to me) and awed by the ice skaters below. I watched the Rockettes dance at Radio City Music Hall and thought that they were the most beautiful women in the world. The last stop on our trip was Macy's, and when we got there it seemed as if time slowed down for just a little while. Every single window for an entire city block was decorated in such a way that I could never imagine.

There was snow, and it looked real! There were elves, small animals, boys and girls, presents and Christmas trees! Everything moved, and I could hardly take it all in. My heart was beating faster in my chest as I tried to take in every little detail of every single nook and cranny in front of me. I remember it was cold, as winters usually are in New York, standing between those big buildings with the wind blowing between. The air was crisp and smelled like roasted chestnuts. I wished that I had a bag to warm my hands, but it didn't really matter. I was happy to just stand there with my friends and watch. And then, finally, my teacher jostled us along, telling us that it was time to go. We all put up a fuss but knew that she was right. We had parents waiting at home, and as much as we hated to admit it, it was cold and we had lunchboxes that our moms had packed for us waiting on the warm bus.

As the bus maneuvered its way through the crowded city streets of Manhattan, I could still smell those chestnuts, and to this day I associate that smell with that day long ago when I became enchanted with Christmas. I didn't know it then, but that was the day I found the magic that all of you in Fort Wayne have known about for generations. I saw that magic again in my daughter's eyes the day I watched her as my friend, Donna McEvoy, sat with her and told her stories of WanDerland and a talking Christmas tree. Donna told her stories about Wee Willie WanD and the Santa Train and all of those wonderful windows. After that, Erika was on a mission.

Always on the prowl for a good W&D story, she began to question every person she assumed was old enough to know anything about the W&D period in Fort Wayne. This had the potential to be somewhat embarrassing. The more stories she collected, the more curious Erika became, which led to many trips to local antique shops, where Erika amassed quite a nice little cache of goodies. She even met some W&D celebrities, such as the son of Wolf and Dessauer's "Pie Lady" and numerous former co-workers who had worked in various departments at the store.

From that point, what started out as a child's fascination snowballed into a newspaper article, which was followed by scores of phone calls to us by the people who read it. It seemed as though the people of Fort Wayne and the surrounding areas were thrilled to think that someone so young would have an interest in a place that held so many of their own wonderful memories. These phone calls eventually led to requests for Erika to speak at club meetings and other events. With the snowball growing bigger by the day, we knew that we were not alone in wanting to preserve these memories.

W&D may be physically gone from us, but it will never disappear from the heart of Fort Wayne. Like any city, the people are its heart. Erika was about eight years old when this project got started and she first heard the stories. She's seventeen now, and like most parents, we sigh and think about how fast the time is flying by. To this end, we partially dedicate this work to Erika and to the childlike sense of wonder that the memories of Wolf and Dessauer inspire in us all.

A SHORT HISTORY OF WOLF AND DESSAUER

It was 1896, the year Henry Ford ran his first motor car in Detroit and the year that the Wolf and Dessauer Department Store opened its doors to the people of Fort Wayne. The department store had modest roots, beginning as a two-story, twelve-thousand-square-foot building located at 70–72 Calhoun Street in Fort Wayne, Indiana. It was staffed with thirteen salespeople and was the vision of Mr. Sam Wolf and Mr. Myron E. Dessauer.

The building leased by Wolf and Dessauer was formerly occupied by the Dittoe Grocery Company and the Peter Certia Sample Room. Wolf and Dessauer, wanting to make their store more of a standout than any other of the time, planned to merge the two stores into one larger store and remodel them to include a large plate-glass storefront. It would have many new interior decorations to set their store apart from any other in the city.

Sam Wolf was the son of A. Wolf, who was a Fort Wayne city councilman. He had attended public schools in Fort Wayne, worked as a stamp clerk in the Fort Wayne Post Office and then began his career in retail at the Louis Wolf Store, where he became involved in management. While researching Mr. Wolf, we got the impression that he became a prominent businessman with financial standing enough to take on such an endeavor. It would appear that Mr. Wolf was relatively young when he joined with Myron Dessauer and became involved in the business venture that would become a legend in retail throughout Indiana.

Myron E. Dessauer originally came to Fort Wayne from Montrose, Pennsylvania, and married shortly thereafter. We noted in the first years of the business that Mr. Wolf and Mr. Dessauer invested about $40,000 to begin their store and that they took frequent business trips to New York to

Wolf and Dessauer as we remember it. *Courtesy of Ken Lucas.*

Another view of Wolf and Dessauer. *Courtesy of Ken Lucas.*

buy stock. This allowed them to carry the latest in goods and fashion, which made the store not only a popular place to shop but also a place to browse and meet with neighbors and friends to chat over the wonderful displays. This tradition would carry on over the next eighty years.

The Wolf and Dessauer store became the only dry goods salesroom on Berry Street and met with huge success. In fact, it was so successful that in only four years of business, it outgrew its original building. It became apparent that in order for the store to continue to grow, the building would need to grow as well.

The year was 1908, an exciting time of new technology. It was when photography, X-ray and the Wright brothers' experiments with aeronautics were introduced. It was also the year when the people of Fort Wayne eagerly watched the excitement as the new Barnes Building (which later became Fort Wayne National Bank) was built. The building was immense and was originally planned to be an office building. Luckily, good businessmen that they were, Sam and Myron talked the owners of the building into letting them take it over as the new location for their department store. It would be a four-story building comprising fifty-four thousand square feet and would soon earn the title of being the largest retail business in the state of Indiana.

A crowd gathers to watch the flames. *Courtesy of Ken Lucas.*

The smoke billows upward. *Courtesy of Ken Lucas.*

From its very roots, Wolf and Dessauer made customer service one of its most important objectives. Everyone from the janitorial staff to its owners made it their business to make the customer feel special. That is why from the day it opened its doors, the business endeared itself to the people of Fort Wayne. Unlike other stores in the city, this retail emporium was not just a place to shop. It was a friendly respite that welcomed everyone without regard to financial status. Shoppers with a heavy purse, as well as those looking for only the barest of necessities, could come to Wolf and Dessauer and relax in the comfort of the free "resting rooms" and reception areas that were provided for them. Amazingly for the time, Wolf and Dessauer even had telephones installed for the exclusive use of patrons before many people even had them in their own homes. No wonder a trip to Wolf and Dessauer became a social event and one to look forward to. People wore their Sunday best and made it a special occasion. Wolf and Dessauer brought a little bit of sophistication from Paris to Fort Wayne while keeping the small-town, neighborly feel.

This site remained adequate until 1917, when the business had again outgrown its confines. At this time, Mr. Wolf and Mr. Dessauer acquired a property at Calhoun and Washington that had been occupied by the Fox Brothers Furniture Company. The company was going out of business and doing away with its stock. Plans for the space included tearing down the building and replacing it with a huge, six-story, white, terra-cotta building

Where Fort Wayne Shopped

One block from the Keenan Hotel. *Courtesy of Ken Lucas.*

Firefighters extend their ladders to battle the raging fire. *Courtesy of Ken Lucas.*

complete with basement. Excavation and building was set to begin on March 1, 1917, and was to be ready for occupancy sometime in the spring of 1918. Everybody in the state looked forward to what was to become the most modern business structure of the time.

Although the Wolf and Dessauer Department Store was already one of the largest retail establishments in northern Indiana, this new store would house many new departments. It was more unique than any other store of the time. Because of its size and complex blueprints, the building promised sites and products never seen before.

This new site, which gained the nickname of "the white elephant," truly became the hub of downtown retail activity and is where the legend as we know it today really began.

This was an important time in the history of Wolf and Dessauer because it was the time when the firm became incorporated and became more affectionately known as W&D. W&D began to sell some of the controlling interest to a group of Fort Wayne businessmen, including Samuel Smith, J.P. Doody and G. Irving Latz. It was Latz whose name became most prominently associated with W&D in the coming years.

Under the leadership of Mr. Latz, the store continued to expand, and W&D became one of the most important stores not only in Indiana but also

Flooded Fort Wayne streets. *Courtesy of Ken Lucas.*

Where Fort Wayne Shopped

Right: Firefighters work through the night. *Courtesy of Ken Lucas.*

Below: The white elephant continues to smolder. *Courtesy of Ken Lucas.*

the entire country. In 1920, Mr. Latz formulated what he called the "basis for our relationship with customers and the community":

- "To build a store that will be a credit to the community which it serves."
- "To foster a fine relationship between the store, its customers, co-workers and suppliers."
- "To maintain quality and always sell merchandise at a fair price."
- "To consider no transaction closed until the article purchased has rendered satisfaction."
- "To measure success only by the services which it is able to render to its customers."

This philosophy was enforced and carried out by all co-workers.

W&D stayed at this site for forty-one years and had expanded to the point where it eventually occupied the entire block along the north side of Washington from Calhoun to Clinton Street. It is interesting to note that while researching this book, no one we asked could agree on where W&D was located. Some people weren't sure where it was, and the reason is not just because it moved so many times but rather because, in people's minds, it was just simply "downtown." It was just their main shopping objective.

In 1957, W&D announced that there was to be yet another location. The trend at the time was to locate in the suburbs and stay clear of what appeared to be dwindling businesses downtown. W&D took a stance and bucked this countrywide trend by building downtown anyway. By doing so, it set up the largest downtown Fort Wayne real estate deal up to that time in the city's history.

In 1959, the new site for W&D was a four-story building located on the block bounded by Clinton, Wayne and Barr Street. Sadly, the newly vacant site at Washington and Calhoun would be torn down in 1964 to make way for a parking garage.

Despite meaning progress for the city's future, several landmarks dating back to the 1890s had to be torn down to make way for the new store. These included the Kindle Hotel, the Pape Paint Shop and the Salem Evangelical Reformed Church. A few of the old buildings that the company had constructed along Washington Boulevard remained and were used for the appliance and TV department, the service department and other store offices.

At this point, tragedy struck in the form of a devastating fire. The date was February 10, 1962. The great W&D fire was a catastrophic event that filled the whole downtown area with smoke. Five buildings were either

Another view of one of the largest fires in Fort Wayne history. *Courtesy of Ken Lucas.*

Stroh's Beer. *Courtesy of Ken Lucas.*

A view of the fire from another angle. *Courtesy of Ken Lucas.*

leveled or severely damaged. Sadly, the crowds that gathered to see what was happening actually hampered the firefighters' work. The bitter cold of that February day turned the water necessary to fight the fire into ice, even as it came out of the hoses. Even so, the tireless efforts of the Fort Wayne firefighters prevailed, with the full force of the department being on the scene for more than twelve hours. Some rested for only a brief period, only to return a few hours later until the fire was resolved.

It was reported that the fire chief of the time, Howard Blanton, said, "It wasn't until nine thirty on Saturday night that the fire was brought under complete control." This fire was reported by the *Journal Gazette* to be a multimillion-dollar disaster. It was touted to be the most devastating fire in the city's history, needing 3 million gallons of water to put it out.

Interestingly enough, we did find a fact involving another fire. While looking through a fire department yearbook, there was a photograph of a funeral and a caption underneath that said that it was the funeral of a fireman who lost his life in the 1910 Wolf and Dessauer fire. No one we spoke to had any information to share, but we mention it here for the sake of completeness.

In the interest of being thorough in our research, it is important to note that in 1952 a W&D store was opened in Huntington and was run by William Latz, who was the son of G. Irving Latz. The site was closed in 1969 due to the opening of the South Town Mall store that same year.

The demise of W&D was its sale, first by City Stores and then by L.S. Ayers on December 2, 1969. The beloved store was forced to give way to the retail trend that had spelled the death of downtown Fort Wayne and many other cities in the country: the mall.

KEY PLAYERS

G. IRVING LATZ

A sound merchandising policy has made this a good store. A fine relationship between customer and co-workers has made it a great store!
—*G. Irving Latz*

While researching this book we had the pleasure of meeting the two sons of Mr. Latz, G. Irving Latz II and William Latz of Fort Wayne. The time we spent with them during the interview was memorable because we came away with such a very clear picture of their father, the man who embodied all that W&D was.

Mr. G. Irving Latz started in the retail business at the age of thirteen. He first came to Fort Wayne from New York in 1915 and on January 15, 1916, married Miss Carrie Stiefel. Carrie was a beautiful and well-known socialite of the day who lived with her parents at 1237 West Wayne Street. The couple was married at noon at the home of the bride's parents, Mr. and Mrs. Louis Stiefel. They then set off on a wedding trip back east to New York and Maryland.

With a beautiful wife and a new career before him, the move to manage the ready-to-wear department at Frank's Dry Goods seemed to be a good one, but it was just the beginning. Publicists for Frank's made big news of the arrival of Mr. Latz to Fort Wayne and saw his coming as a chance to increase business. The store's management also saw it as a chance to change some of the old policies at Frank's and to bring in some new life and ideas.

Frank's Store, as it was sometimes called, had been *the* place for ladies to shop in northeast Indiana for a number of years. Frank's was smart enough to capitalize on that by placing ads in the ladies sections of the newspapers announcing that Mr. Latz would be joining the staff, touting his years of buying experience for some of the greatest ready-to-wear stores in New York and Boston.

We don't know if Wolf and Dessauer tempted Mr. Latz away from Frank's, but knowing how smart Sam Wolf and Myron Dessauer were and what sharp business sense they had, it would be hard to believe that they didn't. Seeing such a knowledgeable and capable young man working for their competition, we speculate that they made him an offer he couldn't refuse.

In 1917, Mr. Latz joined the Wolf and Dessauer staff in the ready-to-wear department and, two years later, was promoted to secretary and general manager. It was during his time as an officer at Wolf and Dessauer that he, along with the others mentioned previously in the first chapter, actually purchased the store.

Mr. Latz was described by those who knew him as "a natural born retailer" and as "someone who could just look at an item and be able to tell if it would sell," For example, when angora sweaters were popular, Wolf and Dessauer had them stocked to the rafters.

G. Irving II and William told us that their father had a seventh-grade education and yet he could write full-page editorials that were perfect to the letter. Called a genius by some, most said that one of his most prized qualities was his ability to encourage loyalty in others. He admired class and anyone who was successful in legitimate, honest business. Wolf and Dessauer was a true reflection of the man himself.

When you are a fixture in the community for as long as Wolf and Dessauer, you ride the ups and downs of society, and hopefully you come out on top. One story that illustrates this happened during the Great Depression and was relayed to us by Mr. Latz's sons. During these hard times, Mr. Latz was forced to cut salaries in order for people to keep their jobs at Wolf and Dessauer. Unlike what one would think of most CEOs or general managers, the first salary he cut was his own.

Sadly, he did have to cut other salaries as well, most by 50 percent. But at a time when so many in the country were unemployed, the people at Wolf and Dessauer kept their jobs. When the depression was over and the store was back on its feet, this man of integrity at the helm of the ship paid everybody the money that they would have made if their salary hadn't been cut. His son William summed it up by simply saying, "He gave his best and expected everyone else to give their best, too." From that simple policy grew decades of hard work, respect and loyalty from all of the co-workers who had the privilege of working with Mr. Latz.

Where Fort Wayne Shopped

According to G. Irving Latz II (also known as Bud), in his father's world "the determination of whether or not an item lived up to its expectation was NOT made by the manufacturer's guarantee it carried. It was determined by the customer who bought it. That was unheard of at the time."

Customers loved to see Mr. Latz as he made his daily rounds throughout the departments of the store. His presence was reassuring and comforting to both co-workers and customers. The store policies that he instituted were so innovative that they seem foreign to us even today.

A customer relations department was set up to handle returns. Bud Latz told us, "According to our statistics at the time, our return rate was no greater than other stores in the country, but our customer service was outstanding. It was our best advertising." He continued: "We handled refunds and exchanges on items we knew were abused and sometimes weren't even bought at our store. 'The customer is always right' was a distilled version of my Dad's policy."

What was even more astonishing than the great benefits the customer had when choosing to shop at Wolf and Dessauer was the benefit package that Mr. Latz put together for the people who were lucky enough to work for W&D. Mr. Latz was the first merchant in Fort Wayne to give his workers a five-day workweek. He also established a "Progress Committee" that was composed of representatives from each floor that aired any co-worker complaints. Management always listened, and a correction of the problem came quickly. One week of winter and two weeks of summer vacation after fifteen years of service and then two weeks of each after twenty years of service. Wolf and Dessauer had a pension system and a co-worker discount. Wolf and Dessauer also instituted overtime pay and enabled co-workers to become stockholders in the store's credit union, among many other company perks.

Mr. Latz was also quite civic-minded. Along with other businessmen, he was instrumental in providing the financial backing that brought the Philharmonic to Fort Wayne. He also introduced the concept of the "Community Chest," which was the forerunner of the United Way.

Under his direction, the Wolf and Dessauer Consumer Panel was formed in 1948. The reason was simple. According to a *Journal Gazette* article, Mr. Latz stated, "We want to give the best service possible to the public and feel the best way to do this is to give them what they want." Members of this twenty-three-woman panel met once per month. The panel was composed of interested women and customers who at one time might have expressed dissatisfaction with the store. Mrs. Joseph (Eleanor) Plasket was the hostess, and Chester Leopold, vice-president of advertising and promotion, chaired the panel. Some results of the panel included store opening hours beginning at nine o'clock in the morning instead of ten o'clock, as well as the addition of certain departments and the expansion of some existing ones.

Despite his outgoing community effort and personality, Mr. Latz enjoyed his quiet time, too. He loved to read mystery novels and loved to golf, although according to his sons, he was a "lousy" golfer. When he found the perfect parcel of land to satisfy a long desire to own a farm, he made an offer for 150 beautiful acres. He then began arrangements to purchase them, but the neighbors urged the landowner not to sell because Mr. Latz was Jewish.

In his own classic style, he nonchalantly stated, "If you don't want to sell it to me, then I don't want to buy it from you." As time went on, he and the farmer did become friends, and eventually he did sell the land to Mr. Latz. That property lies in what is now Sycamore Hills in southwest Fort Wayne.

To sum up a man like G. Irving Latz in a few short sentences is impossible. According to son William, "He was not an easy man at home, or at work, but he managed to inspire loyalty and trust in those he came in contact with." We think he inspired more, such as admiration, friendship, accountability and respect.

Our favorite story involves one told to us by William: "One very cold Christmas season, the co-workers came out to the house in truckloads. They had an old piano in one of the trucks to sing Christmas carols to Dad. When they were finished, he invited them all in for hot chocolate. My mother wanted to kill him!"

We wish we could say more about this man who held his family, his work and his community in such high regard. Visiting with his sons and hearing the way they spoke of him made us wish that we could have been fortunate enough to know him. Mr. Latz passed away in 1947 and handed the management of his beloved W&D over to his sons, whose energies certainly would have made him proud. It was an honor to meet his sons, and we can only hope that these few pages have touched the surface of doing their father justice.

The following is what appeared in the March 1, 1947 *Co-Worker* employee magazine regarding the death of Mr. Latz: "The shocking and unexpected death of our great leader came about at Ann Arbor Michigan on Thursday morning, February 13. Mr. Latz had not been feeling well for some time and entered the University Hospital at Ann Arbor for treatment only a week prior to his death. While his passing has greatly saddened all of us, his life and his ideas shall remain a constant challenge and inspiration to us."

Mr. Latz was only fifty-eight years old when he died, much too young to be taken from so many who loved and admired him. He left a wonderful legacy that was proudly continued by all of his family, friends and co-workers.

Since this original writing, we have learned that Bud Latz passed away on February 20, 2008, at the age of eighty-eight. He, like his dad before him, will always be remembered as a pillar of the community and will be sorely missed.

NELSON K. NEIMAN

Mr. Neiman came to Wolf and Dessauer from Texas, where he worked as a manager of Foley's, a large department store in the Houston area. Although not much is known about Mr. Neiman, he was heavily involved as a board member of Junior Achievement and held the office of vice-president of the National Executive Committee. He also held the offices of both vice-president and then president of the National Retail Merchants Association.

Mr. Neiman always believed that Wolf and Dessauer was only as good as its personnel and that the most important retail transaction was the one that took place between the worker and the customer. He was noted to have said, rather frequently, "The finest merchandise and advertising programs are worthless if this last link between customer and store is not satisfactory."

Mr. Neiman married Jane Latz, a worker at the store who later became the fashion coordinator. Their son, Nelson II, became an attorney in Washington, D.C. Their only daughter, Carol Lynn, married Mr. Richard Chalker Jr. and moved to Evanston, Illinois, where she worked for a publishing company. They also had two sons, Cary and Gregg. It's unknown what career turns their lives took, but it is known that Cary went to Yale and was also a worker at Wolf and Dessauer.

At the time of Mr. Neiman's acceptance of the CEO position, it was decided that William S. Latz (Bill), who was then the secretary of Wolf and Dessauer, would be promoted as assistant to the president.

DALE FERGUSON

Mr. Dale Ferguson came to Wolf and Dessauer in 1939 as an "extra" during the Christmas rush. His title was "Assistant to Stock Boy," and even this auspicious title was only gained after sitting for three weeks in the employment office and hearing that there were no jobs available. His tenacity paid off when the employment manager decided that the only way to get rid of him was to hire him.

Interestingly, while young Mr. Ferguson was taking inventory one day, G. Irving Latz peered over his shoulder and said, "Young man, you write so poorly, I predict someday you'll be a buyer." As the story goes, that prediction came true.

Mr. Ferguson left the store to become a pilot in the United States Air Force and then returned in 1945. He was promoted to assistant buyer in linens in the fall of 1946 and was also made budget floor home furnishing buyer. In 1947, a promotion made him the buyer for linens in domestics, and in 1958 he became home furnishings merchandise manager.

In the true Wolf and Dessauer spirit of family, Mr. Ferguson's mom was a retired co-worker, and his wife, Jean, ran the servicemen's counter during the war years. His son, Mike, worked at Wolf and Dessauer during high school.

CHESTER LEOPOLD

As we went about our research for this book, the name "Leopold" kept popping up. Mr. Leopold was the head of the promotions department at Wolf and Dessauer and was responsible for a lot of things that have become Christmas traditions in Fort Wayne.

Although he is no longer living, we were able to get in touch with his son, Chuck. We reached Chuck by telephone at his home in Aiken, South Carolina, and he was very helpful in giving us the information we needed, as well as some insight into the life and personality of the man who decorated Christmas for us all:

> *Jim and Kathie: So Chuck, it's really nice to talk to you. Can you tell us, what was your dad's first name, and where did you guys live in Fort Wayne?*
>
> *Chuck: His name was Chester, and we all lived on Flemming Avenue.*
>
> *JK: What exactly was your dad's job with Wolf and Dessauer?*
>
> *C: He was the promotions director and one of the vice-presidents.*
>
> *JK: Tell me what he was like.*
>
> *C: Dad was very creative. He had a degree in journalism from Syracuse University in New York. He came to Fort Wayne in 1947 from Rochester*

and worked for a large department store there. He also worked for the Hickock Bell Company.

JK: What was it that brought him to Fort Wayne? Was it to take a job with Wolf and Dessauer?

C: Yes, he was offered a job with Wolf and Dessauer as sales promotion director and then later was promoted to a vice-president.

JK: Did Mr. Latz offer him the job?

C: Whoever offered him the job died before my father came. The person who took his place, I think it was Mr. Latz Sr., died, and then store people still wanted him to come. So he did, and then I think it was Nelson Nieman who became the president of the store. I believe it was Bud Latz after that.

JK: How old were you when you made the move to Fort Wayne?

C: I was five years old.

JK: Just a little guy then?

C: Yeah, I was pretty young.

JK: So, was it really your dad that came up with whole Wee Willie WanD idea?

C: My father came up with the idea of Wee Willy WanD, and also one of his artists helped him in designing the character. Her name was Isabelle Parker.

JK: Wasn't she the lady who also helped design the lighted Santa Claus display?

C: Well, that was there before my father came to Fort Wayne, probably in the early '40s, but that's what I've heard.

JK: So, Isabelle Parker helped your dad design Wee Willie WanD. Do you remember what year that was?

C: It was probably around 1950, give or take.

JK: So did your dad also write the Wee Willy WanD story then?

C: Yes. And that was printed in the newspaper every year.

JK: Do you know anything about the manufacturer of Wee Willy WanD?

C: I know that they ordered a bunch of them. When you mentioned Mattel™ in the letter you sent, it rang a bell because I think my father mentioned that. I don't want to give you any incorrect information, but I think that is correct, and I think Wee Willie WanD was sold in a red box.

JK: Do you remember how much they originally sold for?

C: No, Not exactly. I think it was for a buck or so. You know, it wasn't any big deal. The bottom line was it was for sales promotion. Along with Santa Claus and the Santa Claus special and the mechanical windows and the television show, it all went together. There was also a Wee Willie WanD store just for children. Did you know about that?

JK: Yes, the store where only kids could shop.

C: Right. Kids could buy things that were priced very inexpensively, and of course mom and dad would say, "Here's fifty cents," or something like that. Remember, this was the '50s and '60s, and that could buy a lot then. Then the children would go in and buy their stuff. The co-workers would wrap it for them. I think I still have a bag from the WanD shop.

JK: I know. That was a big deal for kids. I remember hearing about it when I was little and seeing it on the TV show, but I never went in. Chuck, do you know if they had different actors playing Wee Willie WanD? I know that since Wee Willie was an elf, they usually wanted a girl to play the part.

C: That's correct. And I think that the person playing the part did change. I don't think there was only one person who did it. As you mentioned in our initial conversation, though, Phil Steigerwald did play Santa every year.

Where Fort Wayne Shopped

JK: Did your dad come up with the whole concept of WanDerland?

C: Yes, he did.

JK: Chuck, for the people who may never have heard of WanDerland, how would you describe it to them?

C: Do you mean the whole Christmas display kind of thing?

JK: Yes.

C: Well, I think he got a lot of the ideas for it by trying to model the advertising for Wolf and Dessauer after the big name department stores of the time. Stores like Neiman Marcus, Saks 5th Avenue, Macy's and Gimbels and the like. He won a lot of awards for this kind of advertising, which put Fort Wayne on a par with New York and Chicago.

Everything always started the evening after Thanksgiving. These days, stores start putting out their Christmas stuff before Halloween is even over, but back then it was different. Christmas was special, and a whole sense of anticipation was built up through the whole season. The whole concept was to get people in the mood to start making their Christmas purchases. They decorated the entire inside of the store and on the outside as well.

JK: Did they add new things to WanDerland every year to keep it fresh and new?

C: Well, yes and no. Of course, Santa and Wee Willie WanD and the WanD store stayed the same, and the TV show did, too. The Santa Claus special was added later. Of course, the window displays were changed every year. It was never the same thing two years in a row. After they did it for one year, Wolf and Dessauer would sell the displays, or parts of the displays, to other stores, and they'd be reused somewhere else.

JK: I'd imagine they'd be pretty collectable. So nobody knows where they are now?

C: I suppose they are probably long gone. When L.S. Ayers bought Wolf and Dessauer, I think they did away with all of that.

JK: Are there any window displays that you especially remember?

C: I can't remember any that really stands out. Of course, there were displays of Santa and the elves and all kinds of little animals getting ready for Christmas. There were little trains going around in circles. You know, that kind of thing.

JK: Did you get to see any of these window displays before the public did since your dad was the one who put them together?

C: I used to go on buying trips to Chicago with him when he purchased them.

JK: You know, it's very difficult to track those things down. They have some mechanical Christmas figures at the Fort Wayne History Center, and they are not 100 percent positive that they're the originals, but they seem to think they are.

C: I could probably look at them tell you if they were or not.

JK: They have about twenty or thirty animated figures there, mostly of little children.

C: Well, that reminds me that there were carolers also. You know, animated ones.

JK: That's what they have here, so maybe they are original.

C: Well it's possible that in the last years of the store they weren't sold back or traded but stashed away somewhere. Maybe when L.S. Ayers bought the store, they found them and just wanted to get rid of them and sold them off to someone.

JK: It sounds like that might be what happened. What was it like the night they unveiled the windows? Was there a ton of people downtown to see this?

C: Oh yes, oh yes. At the old building on Washington and Calhoun, they would block off the streets so people could be there when they turned the windows on. I believe that was the night after Thanksgiving.

JK: How soon did they start working on the windows before they unveiled them?

C: Oh about six months or more ahead of time.

JK: Wow, that's a really good head start!

C: Yep, my father would start working on Christmas in the spring.

JK: Designing and buying?

C: Designing and buying and working with the people in Chicago and coming up with novel ideas. Of course, it would have to be the kind of design that they could manufacture there in the store or send out without too much trouble.

JK: Your dad must have loved his job. It sounds like it was wonderful.

C: Well, he did absolutely love it. He was very serious about it and dedicated to it. It did take its toll on him, though, over the years due to all the pressure, but if he had his choice he wouldn't have done anything else.

JK: How many years did he work at Wolf and Dessauer?

C: I can tell you exactly. He started April 1, 1947, and stayed until L.S. Ayers bought it out. In fact, he stayed on with them a while and even went to Indianapolis for a year before they replaced him in 1972.

JK: Chuck, a little while back you mentioned a Santa Claus special? Can you tell me about that?

C: Sure. It was also called the "North Pole Special." Children would come to Wolf and Dessauer with their parents prior to Thanksgiving and get free tickets for a train that W&D had rented from Pennsylvania Station. The train would take them west of Fort Wayne to one of the little towns, and as it passed by, Santa would be on a caboose waving. The train would stop and turn around, and Santa and Wee Willie WanD would get on the train and ride back to the Fort Wayne station with the kids and their parents.

JK: Wow, the kids must have loved that!

C: It was fun. I rode it myself a couple of times.

JK: Is there anything else you'd like to mention before we wrap up the interview?

C: Have you talked to Phil Steigerwald yet?

JK: Not yet, but we plan to.

C: Well, Phil was the Wolf and Dessauer Santa and served on the city council and sang at churches and the Jewish Temple.

We'd like to thank Mr. Leopold for taking part in this interview. His father was such an important part of Wolf and Dessauer, no work on that topic would really be complete without him.

PHIL STEIGERWALD

Likewise, no memories of Wolf and Dessauer would ever be complete without talking to the man almost everyone in Fort Wayne regarded as the real Santa Claus: Phil Steigerwald. If you watched, as I did, the daily TV show, you know what an integral part Phil played in the Wolf and Dessauer legend. He was involved in real estate and, at the time of this interview, no longer portrayed Santa at public functions, but his memory of when he did is still vivid.

It didn't take too long to track him down, but scheduling the interview by phone took a bit longer. Mr. Steigerwald kept a busy schedule even then, and I'm grateful that he took the time to speak with us. Wolf and Dessauer was a big part of the magic of Christmas in Fort Wayne, and Phil was arguably the force behind that magic.

JK: So Phil, are you a Fort Wayne guy?

Phil: Absolutely.

JK: How long were you employed by Wolf and Dessauer?

Where Fort Wayne Shopped

P: About thirty-five years.

JK: Were you Wolf and Dessauer's first Santa Claus?

P: No, there were several before me. The two most recent that I had knowledge of were friends of mine. One was a gentleman by the name of Joe Higgins. Joe was the sheriff, if you remember, on the Dodge commercials. In fact, the three of us were going to talk about how we're all civic theater people now.

JK: So, you did do some acting then?

P: Oh yeah. Joe Higgins went to California and did all of the Dodge commercials. Then there was Jim Voors just ahead of me. I replaced him, and Jim passed away just this past year. We were all in the theater together, and Jim Voors was more of a professional actor than the rest of us. As a matter of fact, he was in New York as a Shakespearean actor. At one time, Jim ran a small advertising agency here in Fort Wayne, and until his death he ran a small antique store over on Washington in a small house behind his. He sold gorgeous things. At one time, he put together a rodeo here and brought in the star of the TV show Gunsmoke.

JK: So, he really did quite a few things then?

P: Yes, he really did.

JK: Had you ever played Santa before you came to Wolf and Dessauer?

P: Yep, I was at Sears.

JK: How long did you do that?

P: Just for a year or two.

JK: Did you make a grand entrance when they brought you in for the Christmas season?

P: Yes, I did. Now, at Sears, I came in a by a helicopter for those two years, and I'm not putting anyone down, but nobody put the effort into Christmas like Wolf and Dessauer did.

JK: I think very few places in the country put as much effort into Christmas as they did.

P: Yes, my good Jewish friends the Latzes really outdid themselves to bring a good, uh, what I would call Christian holiday to the children of Fort Wayne.

JK: There are a lot of people who would say that Wolf and Dessauer symbolized Christmas in Fort Wayne for many, many years.

P: They absolutely did! We came in to Wolf and Dessauer on a fire truck to the City County Building. Basically, at that time, I was a member of the city council. I would arrive and greet everybody, and we'd sing a couple of Christmas carols and turn the lights on and do those kinds of things.

JK: That must have been a pretty exciting thing for everyone.

P: If you want to look into something pretty interesting, I can't tell you what year it was, you'd have to go through some of the old newspapers in the library. Politically, they changed Santa Claus right in the middle of my arrival all those years. The national press even picked it up, and the headline read, "Fort Wayne Fired Santa Claus!" It was all over in the newspapers. I never felt that way about it, though.

JK: Fort Wayne fired Santa Claus?

P: Yeah.

JK: I'm not following. What was it all about?

P: Well, I'm a Republican. I'm treasurer of the Republican Party. Now, in those I was very active as a member of the Fort Wayne City Council. I did this every year, you know, and people recognized me. Well, along came a new mayor who ran against me for city council. His name was Win Moses.

JK: Oh! Ok, I get it.

P: He was a Democrat. He still is a Democrat, and I still see him once in a while and I talk with him. Anyway what I'm getting around to is the newspapers made it into a bigger thing that it was.

Where Fort Wayne Shopped

JK: I see.

P: But it did make the national press.

JK: Now, can you tell me what Breakfast with Santa *was like?*

P: Well, first of all tickets always went on sale the day after Thanksgiving. People would come down to Wolf and Dessauer and wait in line to buy them. They would always sell out the first day. The breakfasts were held on Saturdays before Christmas in the tearoom. The parents could come, and they would bring their children. The parents and grandparents or whoever they wanted to bring as long as they had a ticket. They would start lining up out there early in the morning. At breakfast, they would all come in and sit down, and the tearoom served a gorgeous breakfast. Hillard Gates was there as master of ceremonies. Norm Weidenhoffer played the organ. These are all names that had to do with the breakfast. Engineer John Seimer was there, too. We just chitchatted back and forth, going table to table. We talked to people and took pictures with their children. We just became friends with many of the families.

JK: I remember hearing about Breakfast with Santa. *I'm not from Fort Wayne, I'm from Hamilton, but I heard about it for years, and I always wanted to come down to it. Now I understand that Jane Hersha, who's now on TV 21, assisted on the show at one time as well. I've heard she played Wee Willie WanD once. Is that true?*

P: No, she just assisted getting the kids up to see me.

JK: As best I can recall, the show was called Santa in WanDerland, *wasn't it?*

P: You got it!

JK: I had to search my memory for that. I was just a little guy when the show came on.

P: Now if you want history on that, Wolf and Dessauer always took out a full-page ad in the newspaper just before Thanksgiving about the whole breakfast and everything.

JK: Did they start the TV show at the same time you started playing Santa Claus?

P: No, no, it was already on TV when I started. It was on channel 33 every afternoon five days a week.

JK: One of things I still remember was your phrase, "No peeking!"

P: Joe Higgins started saying that.

JK: I see.

P: I carried it forth in memory of Joe. Joe was a Santa Claus that goes way back. He used to ride the train to Arcola and back with the kids.

JK: Wasn't that called the "Santa Express"?

P: I think that was it, but I was never on it. I came after that.

JK: You didn't do that, then? There must have been a huge audience for Santa in WanDerland.

P: Yes, everyone ran home from school to see if their friends got on the show.

JK: Do you think that was one of the keys to the show's success? Seeing if your friends were going to be on TV?

P: I think it was very important, and I think that absolutely the Latzes, who owned Wolf and Dessauer, did a tremendous job of merchandising. I was just very happy to be of help to them.

JK: My wife and I did a lot of research for this book, and we met the two Latz sons. They were really helpful and very, very nice people.

P: Oh, they are nice people. They're wonderful people.

JK: Do you have any idea how many kids you saw on a typical day?

P: I don't know how many in a season, but on a busy day like a Saturday, I might see about three hundred.

JK: Wow! So you worked an eight-hour day?

P: Oh yeah, at least. Seven days a week.

JK: Oh boy. So did you ever get a break?

P: Once in a while, but usually when I did, I was visiting somebody's home helping a child who was sick or something.

JK: Are there any special memories that stand out while doing the show?

P: Oh, there are lots of them. Are you talking about serous things or funny things?

JK: Let's start with some funny things.

P: Well, we had an instance where we had a maze where the children stood and waited in line, and the parents had to stand outside of the maze while the child waited to see Santa Claus. It just so happened that when I looked up at a little boy as he worked his way up to me, I noticed his dad and recognized him as my milkman. And I said to the boy, "Is that your dad over there?" and he answered, "Yes, Santa." I said, "I bet you drink a lot of milk at your house," and he looked up at me with big innocent eyes and said, "Well Santa, we used to drink a lot of milk, but daddy started drinking beer." [Laughs] *There was about one hundred people in line who all broke out laughing.*

JK: And this all happened on the TV show?

P: Yes, right on the show! That absolutely happened on the show! There were things like that all the time. At the same time, besides being Santa, I was also a soloist at the Jewish Temple. Of course, my relationship with the Latz's was very strong. It was just very interesting because I would have people like my good friend Steve Shine, whose name I'm sure you've heard…

JK: Sure.

P: His dad and mom used to bring Stevie down to me. Now today, Steve and I work together in politics.

JK: Right.

P: Now when a child would come up that I would recognize from having been in the temple on Friday night, I would look at him and instead of saying, "Merry Christmas," I would wish him a "Happy Hanukah." That would take them aback about twenty-five feet because I knew they were Jewish, and I also knew their last name and they had no idea how.

JK: That must have been astounding to them, making you seem even more like the real Santa.

P: Yeah, lots of times I knew the next person in line, and I used it to really make them believe.

JK: I'm sure it helped to create that illusion.

P: Well, I was so varied in the things that I was doing in town that I could just call their names out.

JK: What are some other funny things that happened on the show? I remember one time you told a story about Rudolph having a cold.

P: Well, he had the chicken pox once. I told the children to cross their fingers so Rudolph would get rid of them before Christmas. We got rid of them all right! All the kids were going around town with their fingers crossed at my suggestion.

JK: [Laughs] Did you hear from any teachers about that?

P: No. Everybody took it in pretty good shape.

JK: Did you run into any kids who were nervous once they got up for their turn on your lap?

P: Oh sure! Yeah, they'd get halfway there and run the other way sometimes! I can give you an example way back at Sears, where they used to put Santa back in the furniture department on the second floor at the store on Rudisill Boulevard. They would bring the kids up the escalator, and when the kids would see Santa Claus sitting there in the overstuffed chair, they would do one of two things. One, they would run to you or two, they would run away!

Where Fort Wayne Shopped

I remember one mom with a little boy who got off the escalator, and instead of walking toward Santa, this mom took him by the hand and started walking in the other direction. This little kid looked back over his shoulder and yelled, "Hey Santa don't leave. I'll be back after mother goes to the potty!" That's a funny thing that happened. There were a lot of sad things, too.

JK: Tell us about some of those.

P: We've lost lives of small children that finally got in to see me shortly before the holidays.

JK: So you would go to their homes, then, if they were too sick to come to you?

P: Yes.

JK: Did you do that often?

P: Whenever I needed to. One vivid memory I have of that type of thing was a little boy—I can't tell you his name but he lived in New Haven. Chester Leopold came to me one day and wanted to know if I would take my dinner hour and go out and see him because he probably wouldn't be here on Christmas. Well, the Fort Wayne City Police Department drove me there in a squad car and brought the police photographer with me, and we went out there with a car full of presents. The neighbors had put together a big Christmas. I had pictures taken with him on my lap and so on. Well, Christmas got closer, and lo and behold on Christmas morning, the paper had his obituary in there. I have four children of my own. They're up in their thirties and forties now. The point being I took my wife, and we went to Harper's Funeral Home in New Haven to visit the family. They'd never seen me out of uniform. I went in, and they recognized me.

JK: They must have recognized your eyes.

P: Yes.

JK: They must have been shocked. That's quite a story, but you made a difference in a lot of people's lives.

P: I tried to.

JK: I know you have.

P: I don't go anyplace without someone calling me Santa Claus. I just had a recent stay in the hospital, and every nurse who came by called me Santa. It's absolutely continual, even though it's been years.

JK: Everyone still remembers. Did the kids ever bring you any gifts?

P: Yes, I still have some handmade gifts in my office.

JK: You still have them after all these years?

P: I own a real estate company, and I still have stuff here that kids made for me. It's really neat. There was always a little box of candy or some kind of gift for Santa Claus. Besides working at Wolf and Dessauer, I also did private parties—one family who now lives in Syracuse, New York, whose dad used to work for General Electric [and] now works as president of Carrier Corporation. For five years in a row, he flew me there for his family. I'm sure there are other Santas there in the state of New York.

JK: But Phil, you were the only real Santa.

P: Yeah, I was to them.

JK: I was thinking that must have been pretty exciting for the kids who had watched your show to see you at a private event. They would definitely know it was really you. They would be able to tell if you were an imposter.

P: I would do parties of maybe two or three hundred for industries. Things of that nature.

JK: Can you tell me a little about that famous suit you wore?

P: Well, the original suit that I wore was originally made for Wolf and Dessauer. It was made before I got there. A seamstress made it, and I think I wore out two or three of them that were copied over the period of years that I was there. I still have it in my closet. I don't use it for anything. It's just hanging there.

Where Fort Wayne Shopped

JK: I did want to ask you if you still had occasion to wear it.

P: No. Going back a few years, I lost a leg, and I decided that was my last year as Santa. I then sent out a hundred or so nice letters to people I had visited over the years to explain to them that I wasn't going to do it anymore and that they should make other plans. I did enjoy being with them, though.

JK: We know how much everyone loved Wolf and Dessauer, but in your opinion, what do you think made it such a great store? There were so many people with so many amazing memories. What do you think?

P: There were several things that made it very special. There were, of course, the windows with the little dolls and the marionettes and everything in them. That made it special. Then there were the men who dedicated themselves to decorating Wolf and Dessauer. Men like Walter Tharp. Walter lived in Fort Wayne, and he put many of the decorations together. When I say "decorations," I mean the big post in the center of the old store. All the decorations made it Christmas. Then they also promoted Santa Claus. This drew people downtown when it really was downtown. Later, of course, the malls came with a Santa in each store. Every one of them was dressed differently, and each of them was dressed wrong. I went down to South Town Mall back when it was booming. I saw Santa Claus in there with his red coat on and plaid pants! That was way out, but these larger companies just don't care.

JK: That was what was so great about watching Santa in WanDerland. You knew you were going to see the real Santa.

P: Well, children could go in there with a dollar and buy their parents their presents all wrapped up.

JK: That was at the Wee Willie WanD store, right?

P: That's right. They could keep the gift till Christmas and give it to their parents, and the parents wouldn't have had to do anything about it.

JK: Do you remember the Wee Willie WanD dolls?

P: Oh sure. I haven't seen one on a long time.

JK: They're still out there. It's really great when you find one. I heard you mention once that the Mattel™ Company made the dolls. Is that right?

P: Yes, that's how I know it to be true.

JK: Let me ask you just a couple of more questions. How did you feel when the store closed?

P: If you're in the theater and you've been doing a show, and you had a good part in it and enjoyed it, when the curtain came down for the last show, that's how it felt.

JK: Who bought the store?

P: First of all it was sold to a company called City Stores. Then it was sold to L.S. Ayers.

JK: Do you remember your last day there?

P: Oh yes, yep, that's when I bought the Santa costume that was left.

JK: I suppose when the store closed there were a lot of tears.

P: Yea, there really were, but the downtown was fading rapidly. There was nothing to do to save it.

JK: Well, Phil, thanks so much for talking to me. You were such a big part of it all, and this has been such a pleasure.

P: You're welcome. I appreciate that.

After this interview with Phil, we were really intrigued with what he told us about the city council "Firing Santa Claus," so we looked into it a little further. When Wolf and Dessauer was closed in 1969, it became even more important for Santa to continue to be a strong force in the lives of the community children. As he told us, Phil continued as Santa for parties and for the annual tree lighting ceremonies downtown. He became an integral part of the celebration, and the community would turn out in droves to see the "real" Santa preside over the holiday once again.

One year, though, all of that changed significantly and did make the national news. The headline in the *Indianapolis Star* on December 15, 1985, read "The Day Fort Wayne Fired Santa Claus." It started a firestorm of impassioned letters to the editor of Fort Wayne's newspapers.

The incident took place around the annual lighting ceremony traditionally held the night before Thanksgiving. This particular year, it was cold, wet and nasty. Sometime earlier in the month, city officials and various other people in positions of authority decided that the usual $100 stipend paid to Phil each year for his services was too expensive. Since at the time the city administrators were putting a lot of effort into promoting the children's zoo, they decided that the Mr. and Mrs. Claus at the zoo would not only fit the bill for the lighting ceremony but would also give publicity to the zoo. The fact that they would do it free of charge didn't hurt either. So it was decided that they would go ahead with this idea and it would be a winner, but they couldn't have been more wrong.

According to the account in the *Indianapolis Star* the next day, at least five sponsors, including a Fort Wayne radio station, had offered to pay the $100 fee so Phil could perform his duties, but Phil went on record to say that he would have done it for free if any would have asked him. He was very hurt, thinking it all political and petty and that it did nothing but hurt the children.

In the end, the whole night went haywire. Mr. and Mrs. Claus from the zoo were involved in a traffic accident just hours before the ceremony was to begin, so the captain of the Fort Wayne traffic division was asked to fill in. Six-foot-two-inches-tall, 230-pound Martin Bender had to get a costume fast! The city committee still did not ask Phil to step in to help. Nor did the members see themselves in any way as villains and maintained that it was not political at all, saying that they only wanted to promote the zoo.

Despite all that happened, a very nice result came of it and started a new tradition for Phil. After hearing about the committee's plan to hire a different Santa, a group of Fort Wayne business men got together and made it possible for Phil, as Santa, to visit all three of the city's children's hospital wards that night. While things were running amuck downtown, Phil was able to bring joy and spread his special brand of Christmas magic to those who needed it most. To him, that's all that mattered anyway.

While doing our research, we also talked to Phil Steigerwald Jr., who was able to give us some more valuable insight about his dad. Phil remembered his father lovingly, telling us that he was a wonderful man who provided a secure home in which he and his three sisters grew up happily.

Phil and his sisters always accepted that Christmas Eve was a "working day" for their dad, and although it felt a little strange at times to share him with so many thousands of other children, looking back, none of them would change a minute of it. They never resented his fame or his popularity. In fact, they even got into the act themselves, each one of them playing the part of Wee Willie WanD at least once at private parties after Wolf and Dessauer closed.

When W&D closed, Phil Jr. likened it to the closing night of a very long-running Broadway show. There were tears for the passing of a part of your life that would never be the same. The curtain came down on Wolf and Dessauer, but Phil, as Santa, lived on. Reprinted here with the permission of Phil Jr. is an actual letter from a Fort Wayne woman. Her name is left off to protect her anonymity:

> *Dear Santa,*
>
> *I just got done reading the article in the newspaper about you. As a child we have several Christmas photos with you and they are cherished. But to our family you will always be the man that was Santa all year long. My mother was a single parent in the sixties, alone with no family from here when there was not much assistance. I was young but I remember as a child my mother crying one year and saying your name. That somehow you had arranged for us to have a Christmas. But now I want to tell you how you were Santa all year long to us.*
>
> *My mother worked two jobs and always wanted a home of her own for her children. No one would help a single parent at the time, but you did. You sold and guided her into being a homeowner. Since then, she has bought three other homes. My mother always said to me, if "Mr. Steigerwald hadn't given me a chance, I don't know where we would be." That's why in our hearts you will always be Santa all year long.*
>
> *For over forty years, your name has been a part of our lives. My mother recently passed away at 86. She always said a small prayer for you, Santa. Now that she is no longer with us, I will continue to thank God for this Christmas miracle that Santa Steigerwald did so long ago. That one kindness changed our lives forever and provided us with the wonderful lives we have today. "Merry Christmas!"*

Many didn't know it, but Phil Steigerwald suffered from diabetes for more than thirty-five years. At the urging of his devoted children, who were concerned for his health, Phil hung up his Santa suit for good when he suffered a below-the-knee amputation due to a nonhealing abscess on his foot. Phil was fitted with an artificial leg and still wanted to make Christmas happen for the city's kids, but his own children prevailed.

Later, Phil's kidneys failed, forcing him to endure four hours of dialysis three days per week. Next it was discovered that his eyesight was failing and that he had developed a heart condition. Despite all of this, Phil continued to run his real estate business from his home and stayed active in the city's political circles. His children took care of him, taking turns preparing his meals right up until the end, when the great man closed his eyes for the last time.

The gentleman who had left his mark on an entire community was gone, leaving a huge void in the hearts of generations. Thinking about Phil, it's important to remember that he was a man of vision and faith. Perhaps remembering his courage, kindness and determination can be the legacy that helps to fill that void. For the sake of his memory, go ahead and picture his face when you tell your little ones about Santa. Think of his twinkling blue eyes when you read them Christmas stories, for if there were ever a "real" Santa, he lived, worked and loved right here in Fort Wayne.

THE LATZ INTERVIEW

The first interview we ever did for this book was an interview with the late Bud and Bill Latz. Their father was G. Irving Latz, the man responsible for a good deal of the success of the Wolf and Dessauer store. These brothers were a delight to talk to, and we probably could have written an entire book based solely on the stories they told us on that cold February night in 2002.

We hope that this interview gives you a little insight into what made the store tick for more than one hundred years and also helps you capture a bit of the spirit of these gentlemen. We started our interview by asking them about the famous Christmas windows.

Bud: The Christmas lights you're talking about that provided such a big memory were in the windows in the store along Washington and Calhoun Street. They brought a lot of people from the small towns down here. Fort Wayne's a big town compared to the small towns around here. Sort of like New York is in that respect.

JK: Oh yes, that's true. It was to me. I remember as a small boy coming down here from Hamilton, and it seemed huge. The thing I remember most about Wolf and Dessauer was watching Santa Claus on television.

Bud: With Hilliard?

JK: Yes, with Hilliard Gates. But I don't remember who was Santa at the time?

Bud: Phil Steigerwald. There were other people playing Santa Claus, but Phil did the job. He was an actor himself. He was a wonderful personality with the kids. He had so much patience and treated each one as a special child.

Bill: Santa Claus used to come in on a train. We would go up to Columbia City and turn around and take everybody on a ride.

Bud: They'd all get on the train, and it was at least a half-hour trip into Fort Wayne. They'd all get off at Pennsylvania Station.

Bill: Then we'd walk up Harrison Street when the weather was nice, and then it was the time for Breakfast with Santa.

Bud: Hilliard Gates helped with that. He was terrific. He had so much energy, and I don't know where it all came from.

JK: That show was broadcast on WKJG, right?

Bill: Yes, and Hilliard was managing the station, and he wouldn't let anyone else do it but him.

JK: Because he wanted it to come off just right?

Bill: Yes.

Bud: Why don't you ask us what you would like to know about the store.

Bill: We could reminisce all day.

Bud: We'd be all over the lot [laughs].

JK: We wanted to ask you about the Wee Willie WanD doll. Was he made by what became the Mattel™ toy company?

Bud: Yes, when they were just a mom and pop operation out of their garage. That is true.

JK: Do you remember what year that was?

Bud: That was Chet Leopold's idea, so that would have been around 1948 or 1949.

Bill: The late 1940s. He started because we were the flagship store with the "real" Santa, and we needed somebody to patrol the floor and round up the kids and get them to sit on Santa's lap, and we didn't know what to do.

Bud: Our public relations guy, Chet Leopold, came up with the idea of Wee Willie WanD, and he was an instant success. His name came from W&D in the same way that our sidewalk café was called "La Baton," which is French for "wand."

JK: That makes sense.

Bill: Well, I don't know if it made sense, but that's what we called it [laughs]. But Christmas downtown was Christmas at Wolf and Dessauer. Of course, it wasn't near as pretentious in the beginning, but it became bigger and bigger and bigger, and the windows became a talking point. People would come downtown on Thanksgiving evening, probably around six o'clock, to see the unveiling of the windows. They would come there in their blankets, and there would be thousands of people. It was a really big thing.

Bud: There were moving toys. They depicted various things in the Christmas story. It wasn't like you took one look at them. Parents were explaining to the kids about what they had read to them. This was unique. Really big.

JK: Now the store moved a few times, didn't it?

Bill: We had two principal places. From 1919 to 1959, we were on the corner of Calhoun and Washington. Then, as the store grew, we took over buildings adjacent to Washington Street. That's the store you see where the buildings were white terra cotta. Then the next store was the Store For Men. That's what our father always called it. Everyone else always called it the Men's Store.

Then we took over the Home Furnishing Store, and then the last store we took over was on the corner of Clinton and Washington was the Appliance Store. That's where we lived until 1959, and then we lost our lease and built a new store, which opened February 2, 1959. It was a very cold day. An interesting sideline: we got a speaker through Read Chapman of CBS. It was Robert Trout, who just died in the past couple of months. And he came out to speak, and he had a wonderful voice.

Bud: Yes, he was a very nice man. A lot of class.

Bill: The reason I brought that up was to me, I was thinking tonight while I was driving down here. I think what I would like to give is why the store became such a special memory, and I think there are darn good reasons. One of the reasons is Dad's policy of the store, which was completely different than other retailers in Fort Wayne.

This was during the era before discount operations had appeared. This was a bond between an awful lot of shoppers and the store, and it was our Dad that put this into effect. It was a little broader than "the customer is always right," which is the kind of distilled thing of what the policy was. We were handling refunds and exchanges on items we knew darned well were abused, or where the store had been "taken for a ride." But that was Dad's policy, and it really proved quite effective. It made the store more than just a department store.

Bud: What we did, as Bill says, most of the basic rules of the store were set by Dad, and what we did was to carry that on. Briefly, what we said about our merchandise was that it didn't matter what the manufacturer said. The determination of whether or not the goods had done what they were supposed to do was with the customer. It wasn't with us. We had a customer relations department that was set up for you to bring things back, and this was not done generally at that time. We never argued. We took back merchandise that wasn't even ours.

Bill: We just didn't argue. The people that worked there, the co-workers, were instructed not to stand there like, "We're the store, who are you?." We didn't want any of this.

JK: In our research, we found that the customer service at Wolf and Dessauer was just amazing. That is certainly lacking in most stores today.

Where Fort Wayne Shopped

Bud: We had all the statistics at the time. Our returns weren't any greater percentage-wise than around the country. It didn't cost us anything, but it was the best advertising we had. Everyone knew they could buy with impunity. They knew they were going to be determining whether it was right or not. They could bring it back.

Bill: My favorite story, on the first floor where I had some departments that I was buying for, the store would take a certain area and have something that was "hot" there. At one time, we sold books in one of those areas. Novels, nonfiction, whatever was popular. I remember this very well. This woman came back in the midafternoon. I was standing around, and she wanted to return the book she had bought earlier. I asked her why, and she answered, "The title was misleading." [Laughs] It was wonderful that she really thought that the title was wrong and wanted her money back!

Bud: What's your next question? I wanted to get to why the store was so great.

JK: Well, I think your dad was largely the cause of that. I've been hearing so many wonderful things about him, and I think what he did in the store, instituting policies that made average, everyday shoppers feel special, I think that's the major part of why it sticks in the mind of so many people, even today.

Bud: That's true. What he did for the customer he also did for the co-workers. The loyalty of our co-workers was fantastic.

Bill: Some of them were there for thirty years or more.

JK: Wow! That is amazing! You'd never hear of that today!

Bud: This was a guy with a seventh-grade education. Kids at school used to call him "fatty." A very good ready-to-wear person and very good at telling what would sell. That's what started him on his way. His other characteristic that made him an interesting person was that in many ways he was not an easy man. He wasn't the best-educated person, but he had an ability to create loyalty. He admired what he didn't have in life. He admired class in anyone who was very successful in a legitimate business. It made such an impression on us. I know there are story after stories about him, and that's why I keep bringing you back to this. The store was pretty true to a reflection of him. People thought the store was dad [laughs]. What a guy.

Bill: I think the second-biggest thing in his life was the farm he always wanted to own...That was our house. We lived there for eight years, and then, as Bud says, it became the beginning of the clubhouse, and Walter Probst added a heck of a lot to it.

Bud: [Laughs] Yeah, we had 150 acres, and Walter added about 2,000. Part of the home is still standing—the part that was our sister's room.

JK: That was the clubhouse?

Bud: That's right. Anyway, back today.

Bill: We eventually became buyers in the store, and dad was full of this idea that you start at the bottom. He had the idea, "I'm Mr. Latz, and you're Bud and Bill Latz," [laughs] and that kind of established who we were. Periodically, he would call you up to his office. It would scare the pants off you, to meet whoever was up there that he figured would help you out later in life. He did this with me several times. Sometimes the people would turn out to be lifelong friends that you might not otherwise have had the chance to meet.

Bud: One time, we had to go down to lunch at the chamber. It was the beginning of Alpo. It was horrible food [laughs]. I didn't see any reason to go down there except he said, "You be down there." He gave a talk. I don't think it lasted fifteen minutes. That talk was the beginning of the Community Chest, which was the forerunner of the United Way. Just an idea of dad's as a businessman who thought that all of these agencies that would come in and interrupt your daily life should be combined into one final effort once per year. From there was about a half-dozen businessmen that joined.

Bill: That really set the pace for the town. There was Charlie Bushing, the head of the bank. I could go down the list and tell you these people. Dad with his education and those men who didn't have much more education were very successful. The best example was that they realized that this town had to have everything it needed to make it successful.

Where Fort Wayne Shopped

Frank Lymen started the Philharmonic. He started it because he loved music, but dad was in that group with Charlie Bushing that gave the money that helped start it. My dad I don't think ever went to a serious music thing in his life. He just didn't enjoy it. He read mystery stories. He loved to play golf. A lousy golfer! But he loved to play. He loved to walk all over the farm. He was something else.

Bud: When we first got into the store, we were selling. I was in furnishings. It was a big department. It was around Christmastime, and I remember dad walking through the store at least once a day. You didn't know when, but you were quite alert when he went through. He expected you to look like you just came out of the shower or something like that. He was meticulous about his grooming and clothes.

Bill: Yes, that's right. He was meticulous.

Bud: At that time, there was a collar you could buy for men's shirts that was a stiff collar that was detachable. It had a collar button in back, and it looked spiff all day. Well, he scared me so much that I bought a box of those collars so that I would look "band box" most of the day. You didn't have "Dr. Laura"–type talks with dad. There was none of that.

Bill: One thing neat about the store was that it wasn't only outside. We decorated the inside like that, too, and there were people singing carols and music playing. The day before Christmas, dad stood at the door and gave everybody a box of chocolates and a handshake. He'd wish them Merry Christmas. It would take about an hour or two to get through everyone, and at that time of the year he was busy. But doing that meant something to him and meant something to those people.

JK: Sure, I'll bet it meant a lot.

Bud: The other thing that Bill mentioned is very important. Dad was in that store all of the time. Not in his office. He walked that store, and everyone else knew it. You would see our father a lot, and it made people feel good that he had that kind of interest in how they were being served. He was a real merchant. He was a good businessman. He could go in your department and tell you what was selling. He was the kind of merchant you don't see a lot of today. He would go out and buy like ten items and sell them. When he found something that was a hit, he would stock up like crazy. I remember when angora sweaters were the most popular things that season; we saw so much angora!

Bill: *Dad had a great sense of humor, too. One of his favorite things was to put you with the most awful buyers.*

Bud: *Oh yes. One guy I had was from New York, and this guy was sharp. I couldn't imagine why I was with this guy. He was doing everything wrong, against the policy. Like when a lady would come in, and nothing was right for her, he would go into his little cubbyhole and hid and send me out to take care of things. He didn't even try to help, and this went on until over the weekend, when I went to dad and said, "Hey Dad, you got a live one here, this guy you put me with." Dad had a great laugh at the stuff I was telling him and said, "Don't you get it? You'll learn faster from these people than from people who do it right." Dad knew how this guy was. You couldn't pull the wool over his eyes.*

Bill: *There were other community things, too. In those days, they still had orphans and orphans' homes.*

Bud: *Once a year, Dad would host a special dinner. They served the same dinner every year. Chicken and noodles. We all served them—us, the buyers. These kids never got out, so they loved it. They could eat all they wanted.*

Bill: *These days, people would look at that and say, "How condescending!" At the time, though, it was pretty unique. Dad's whole philosophy was to help when he could. The kids would eat like they never ate before. The kids just loved it.*

JK: *I was also reading about your dad and the store policies he instituted with the co-workers and the different benefits he gave them.*

Bill: *Yes, they were outstanding for the time.*

JK: *So that was very unusual then?*

Bud: *No, we were one of the first companies to have insurance for our co-workers. Got it through Lincoln Life. Dad was amenable to suggestions, and he really listened. When he thought an idea was good, he would go for*

it and not be afraid to gamble a little with the outcome.
Bill: We could tell you stories that would take up the whole night, but we never put one over on Dad.

JK: I bet your sister got away with more than you two boys ever did.

Bud: Yeah! He loved our sister. She had the best mind in the family. A great retailer. Anyway, he was crazy about her. You know fathers and daughters [laughs].

JK: Yes, dads are like that with their little girls.

Bud: I remember he walked me to school with him every day while he walked to work—1200 West Wayne Street. We would converse, and it was a special time. This guy was so smart. He was a genius. He would write editorials, full-page ads. He'd write editorials on work conditions, national concerns, and they were letter perfect. They were wonderful.
In the Second World War, we took the front window and sold war bonds, $3 million worth. It was maybe Walter Winchell or some other nationally known person had an article about that and the number we had sold. I remember because my dean of students called me out of class to ask me if I had seen the article or knew about it. I hadn't. But it was the only thing that the dean of students ever remembered about me! But that's a whole other interview [laughs]!

Bud: But I'm glad I got you back to dad. If you don't stop bringing up Christmas, we'll be here all night [laughs].

JK: [Laughter] I can't help it. It's so fascinating. So anyway, your dad was the main thing in Wolf and Dessauer in the minds of the customers, right?

Bud: Well, it certainly had a lot to do with it, but it was an exciting time. Christmas was a big deal. Most department stores don't make any money ten months out of the year but make all of their profits from Halloween through Christmas, so we did all of these things. We did them, and we didn't do them in a phony fashion. We didn't try to use religion or religiosity to build our business, but at the same time we knew it was an important activity for us to support. There certainly were a lot of people exchanging gifts!

Bill: That Santa Claus thing, I was there when the one fellow who was the actor played Santa. He was a cop in a TV series. He was the sheriff in that famous commercial. It was a Dodge commercial. He developed a line for them, and he developed a line for us, too. He would tell all the kids, "No peeking!" Kind of like, "Awesome!" is today [laughs].

Bud: [Laughs] And he was interesting. He came back once from Hollywood. Joe Higgins. That was his name. He came back one year just to be Santa, can you imagine!

JK: Wow! Was he from Fort Wayne?

Bill: Well, I don't know if he was a native or not, but he lived here for quite some time.

Bud: He was very successful in civic theater and in Hollywood. His claim to fame was that he played a detective in a show called Detective Story. *Listen, before this becomes* The Forsythe Saga, *I don't know whether we are covering what you want or not* [laughs].

JK: Oh yes, this is great.

Bud: We tend to run in.

JK: No, its been wonderful. We could listen to you talk all night, but we better let you go before the roads get too bad. We can't thank you enough for coming out tonight and for letting us pick your brains like this.

Bill: We've enjoyed ourselves. You let us know if you need anything else.

Bud: Yes, just call. We'll be looking forward to seeing the book when it's finished. This was a lot of fun.

JK: Well thank you again. Your insight is invaluable.

SALLY BROCKMEYER

Shortly after a newspaper article about our daughter, Erika, and her Wolf and Dessauer collection appeared in the newspaper, we got a phone call from a very sweet lady. Sally had worked for Wolf and Dessauer for a long time in the advertising department and had a bunch of old advertisements and things that she had held on to after the store closed. I guess she had been tempted several times to just throw them away, but something always stopped her. Once she learned about Erika, she said that she knew she had found the person who should receive her treasures.

Sally gave us some wonderful ads and a great recipe book. They helped us to round out our research and were so much fun to go through. We give our thanks to Sally for all of her generosity and help.

JK: Sally, what made Wolf and Dessauer different than any other store?

Sally: One thing different that we did was the teen board for high school kids and the college board for girls entering college.

JK: Was that like a special focus group?

S: It was a bunch of girls that were interviewed, and then a program was put on telling them about fashions in high school and what to expect at college.

JK: What would typically be discussed?

S: Oh, what to wear and what good activities there would be to be involved in.

JK: How did that tie in with Wolf and Dessauer? Was it just for public service then?

S: Yes, for public service.

JK: That's interesting. Who was in charge of it?

S: Chester Leopold, my boss.

JK: Well, that's pretty fascinating. Did they invite as many kids as wanted to come.

S: Yes, right. We would put ads in the paper. We had modeling, too, all the new fashions.

JK: Were the models paid?

S: No. It was just something they did.

JK: Did you choose people from the boards to do that?

S: No, not necessarily. We had girls always wanting to be models for us. Some of them we used, but most of them were professional.

JK: I know there were models roaming about the store to show off the latest fashions. Did they do that every day?

S: Well, not every day of the year, but every day of the new fashion seasons. Christmas and so on, back-to-school season. And then we had a Sunbeam Lady who did a lot of cooking demonstrations for us.

JK: I remember those from when I was little. What did she cook?

S: Oh, anything to show how the appliances would work. And then, of course, we had Santa in WanDerland *in the auditorium.*

JK: Tell me about the auditorium. Was it different from the toy department?

S: Well, the toys were on the second floor as I recall. The auditorium was on the fourth floor. I think it was just used for special promotions. They would hold fashion shows. They used it for WanDerland during the holiday season, and different organizations would come in and hold lunches during the year.

JK: What years did you work for Wolf and Dessauer?

S: I started in 1952 and was there until it closed and then became Ayers and left that location in 1992, so I was there for forty years.

Where Fort Wayne Shopped

JK: What was your title, Sally?

S: I was the secretary to promotion director.

JK: What did you do on a typical day?

S: I typed a lot of memos! I did the mail and other basic general secretarial duties. I worked closely with Mr. Leopold. He got a lot of letters.

JK: We talked to his son Chuck, too. He was very helpful in telling us about his dad and how he impacted the store. What was your favorite time of year to work at the store?

S: Christmas was always fun and the busiest, watching the windows get set up.

JK: How long before Christmas did they start working on the windows?

S: I'd say about three months. Windows were draped for about three weeks or more so people couldn't see them. We wanted it all to be a surprise.

JK: What was your favorite thing about Wolf and Dessauer?

S: The people. They were all very people-oriented and wanted everyone to be happy. Mr. Leopold was wonderful. He was a wonderful man.

JK: You kept a lot of newspaper ads. What was the reason you saved them?

S: I kept them because I knew when the store closed it would all be gone forever. I couldn't make myself part with them. I knew someone would want them someday.

JK: They are wonderful. They were such a big part in helping us to write this book. Does anything else stand out in your mind about your years there?

S: Well, Christmastime will always stand out. I remember Santa had about three different suits. It was my job to take them to the cleaners to get them cleaned. I'd lug them down the road all the time. It was a fun job, though.

JK: Did you work with Phil Steigerwald?

S: Well, we saw that he got his meals. He worked long hours.

JK: In your department, sales promotion, what other things did you do? What promotions did you do when you weren't working on Christmas stuff?

S: Back-to-school was a big one.

JK: Since I'm a radio guy, I wanted to ask, did you ever work setting up radio remotes or anything like that?

S: Mr. Leopold did. We worked with WOWO a lot. Mostly advertising new products, but they would come down to WanDerland when Santa was there every year and talk to the children.

JK: Tell me about the "Santa Express."

S: That was the train that went to Columbia City. After the first time they did it, they didn't think it would be any big thing, but it was so successful that they had to keep adding cars each year. They never had enough to take everyone. It was a huge promotion! Mrs. Claus was on the train with the kids, too. She would talk to the children. That train was a big deal.

JK: Tell me more about the ads.

S: Well, we had copywriters, artists and finish artists. Isabelle Parker was the best artist we had.

JK: Was Wolf and Dessauer a place for people to just come and meet up with each other?

S: Oh yes. It was the place to be. People would meet and come to eat in the cafeteria in the basement or in the tearoom.

JK: Do you think that to work there was a status symbol of sorts?

S: Oh yes. It was a prestigious place to work. People always got a wonderful reception there, and they were confident that we would always take care of their problems.

JK: Can you tell me about some other people who worked there that were special to you? I know you mentioned it was the people who made the place what it was.

S: We had a copywriter that became a great friend of mine. I made a lot of good friends there.

JK: When you took your breaks, did you stay in the store?

S: Mostly we went to the cafeteria or the Trolley Bar.

JK: What kind of things did they serve in the tearoom? Any special dishes they were known for?

S: Nice lunch dishes. I can't think of any off the top of my head.

JK: Can you describe what it looked like?

S: Well, there were tables on either side. You would go in through the line. Usually, women went to the right and men went to the left. [Laughs] I don't know why; they just did. It was a nice place.

JK: We know there was a library there because we found some books in an antique store with a label on them that said, "W&D rental library." Do you know anything about that?

S: No. I didn't know about that. It must have been before my time I guess.

JK: What was it like when you knew the store was going to close?

S: That was a sad, sad time. People cried. It was so sad. But I went to the South Town Mall store when Ayers bought it.

JK: It changed a lot when Ayers took over, didn't it?

S: Oh yes, it changed a lot.

JK: Did they retain a lot of employees?

S: Yes, me for one. They tried to keep as many as they could. They were good about that. Some went to the Glenbrook store.

JK: Well, Sally, thanks so much for everything you have done for us—all the ad prints you sent to Erika and the great recipe book. You've been so helpful. We can't thank you enough.

S: Well, I don't know if I was very helpful tonight, but it was fun.

In summary, we have to thank Sally for her participation in this book. The insight given to us by people like her made writing this book a true pleasure.

CHRISTMAS AT
WOLF AND DESSAUER

C ertainly, any book about Wolf and Dessauer would not be complete without including a section on Christmas. Wolf and Dessauer was the embodiment of the season to so many residents of northeast Indiana, but especially so to the people of Fort Wayne.

We can't tell you how many times we've heard stories of Christmas recollections. Most included memories of standing outside on those cold November nights waiting with delighted anticipation for the unveiling of the window displays. Whole families stood outside in the cold, two or three rows deep. Sometimes the wait lasted hours, but this was one time when no one grumbled and everyone waited with good cheer despite the cold.

Even though that time has passed us by, we can still experience a little piece of what it might have been like by heading downtown around Thanksgiving time, when the lighting of the Santa Claus display takes place. On that night, hundreds of Fort Wayne residents recapture a bit of their past as they wait for the famous countdown to begin and the memories to come flooding back. If you look around the crowd, you can see grandparents and great-grandparents holding the hands of youngsters, maybe a little misty-eyed wishing that Christmas now could be more like Christmas then. But still, while waiting for the countdown, one tradition stands as it was decades ago. On that night, hundreds of Fort Wayne residents do manage to pass on a bit of their past to their families waiting in line to buy Coney Dogs at the famous downtown Coney Island Hot Dog Stand. While waiting in that line that wraps around the block, we've often thought of what it must have been like waiting for those windows to be unveiled at W&D.

We all know that children are used to waiting around Christmas. They start waiting for their gifts and for Santa Claus to come just about as soon as Halloween ends. That anticipation is part of what makes the season so special and so magical for children. That's why the memories linger into adulthood and why we all get so nostalgic around the holidays. That's what this chapter is all about. We're trying to bring back some of those memories.

CHRISTMAS ON DISPLAY

Although other stores in downtown Fort Wayne decorated their windows for Christmas, anyone who ever saw the window displays at Wolf and Dessauer knew that they were beyond compare. People marveled at the detail that went into each creation. Any given year, you would see Santa feeding his reindeer, ice skating raccoons and elves jumping rope.

What really made these so special wasn't just the Christmas theme but rather the delicate movements of these small creatures. The animation, compared

A lovely Christmas scene, brought to life in the W&D windows. *Courtesy of Walter Tharp.*

Where Fort Wayne Shopped

A sleepy-time Christmas Eve for the little ones. This window was designed by Mr. Walter Tharp. *Authors' collection.*

to today, might seem a little dated, but at the time it was cutting-edge and no detail was spared in making the displays more spectacular every year.

The man in charge of those displays from 1928 until his retirement in 1956 was Alan Bixby. Mr. Bixby started his career in retail as an elevator operator in Kalamazoo, Michigan. Window displays at that time were extremely important because they were primary advertisements to get people into the store. At various times during the year, the windows would change with the seasons. For example, at Easter, you would see Easter bonnets, lilies and even live baby chicks.

Bixby would often travel to Marshall Field's in Chicago to study its displays and get ideas to bring back to Fort Wayne. Because he did this, W&D was on the inside track to some of the most amazing ideas in animatronics during the time. The general opinion was that the W&D windows rivaled any that you might see in New York or Chicago.

In our search to locate original W&D animated window display figures, we learned a few interesting things. First, we found that it is really difficult to find them! After scouring area antique stores, we learned why. The reason is because the same figures didn't appear every year. There was such a great demand for extravagant window displays in other large department stores that they would often trade displays or buy them outright. This may have been the case when W&D knew of its coming demise: it might have sold all of its displays off to one of these companies. This would be theory one.

On one occasion during a shopping trip, we found an animated Santa with a broken nose. The seller touted it as being an original W&D window figure. The Santa had a price tag of $300 and carried with it no proof that it ever actually appeared in a W&D window, only the seller's word. When we asked where she had obtained it to try to verify its authenticity, the seller got increasingly angry with each question, so we decided that purchasing the Santa was not the best idea. We've found that most people assume that if something is old, Christmas-related and moves that it must be a Wolf and Dessauer original. We'll learn more about that later, but we have to say that this is not the case.

At the time of the first writing of this book, the closest we probably came to a W&D figure was right here in our own history center. Near Christmas, its staff had set up a large room of moving Christmas figures that they try to do every year. These figures looked like beautifully dressed dolls, some wearing nightclothes and some wearing fancy dresses. The story goes that a man found them in a warehouse and donated them to the history center. It is believed that at one time or another the figures did appear in the store's window.

Possible theory number two is what we call "the warehouse theory." Since writing this new book, we have heard from a second source, a Fort Wayne resident by the name of Chris Shatto who made a W&D find at a local auction in the summer of 2006. What was found was a box of W&D Christmas display items, also said to have come from a warehouse. In the box of items were three Christmas elves in a state of disrepair, a silver tree with color wheel and various other decorations. Chris also relayed to us that there were also three wise men that a church on Crescent Avenue purchased. What supports the warehouse theory for us is the fact that these elves were made by the Sylvestri company. We learned from Walter Tharp, W&D's display director, that Sylvestri is the company that made all of the W&D animated window items. Chris put a lot of money and time into restoring the elves to their former beauty.

As you know, Erika was steadfast about adding a window figure to her collection, and having one of these little guys from the window displays would have thrilled her, but we never were able to find one. That zeal of hers sent us on some fun adventures, as well as some we would like to forget.

One day, after coming home from a very busy day of running errands, I was so happy to plop down on the couch to rest. I must have been there for all of ten minutes when Erika, who was about ten or eleven at the time, came flying down the stairs yelling, "Mom, Mom, get up, get up!" My first thought was that the house must be on fire, but I was soon proven wrong. Erika had listened to our phone messages, and apparently the impossible had happened.

A woman from a church school had called to tell us that she and others had been cleaning out their storage areas and getting rid of a lot of stuff that they had been holding on to for years. The woman went on to say that some of the things they were disposing of were items from W&D (which she said was confirmed by a person who worked at the school who used to work at W&D). She said that they had called the history center first, but they suggested she call us. There was one catch, however. The caller said if we didn't hurry, they'd be thrown away. Since we had been out all day, I was pretty sure that they would be in the trash by the time we got there.

Well, sure enough. We drove down to the church in our old station wagon and saw two old dumpsters. We were told to look for a reindeer, and boy did we see one! I love digging though cobwebs, musty old boxes at flea markets and old, forgotten barns, but I had never gone on a dumpster dive. I looked at the Christmas stuff, half buried in garbage, and then at Erika's face all rosy and happy and figured, "Oh, what the heck!" I rolled up my sleeves and decided to go for it.

The first problem was that the dumpster was huge; in fact, it was taller than I was, so I had to pull the car over to it so that I could stand on it. Upon closer inspection, and by holding my nose, I could see a very large reindeer, a small bent-over boy with a Christmas tree and an old gnome-like figure. All three were tangled in strings of Christmas lights, remnants from elementary school storage rooms and large bags of smelly garbage.

The closest to me was the Christmas tree, so I reached in and made a grab for it. I gave one of the branches a good tug, and the tree came out with relative ease. On the ground it looked okay, about three feet tall, with some small lights and an old electrical cord still attached. It did look old. Back to the dumpster I went, for the bent-over boy next. He was dressed in pants and a sweater, and once he was on the ground, we could see that he was bent over because he was supposed to be tying his boots or ice skates. He had some paint chips missing and was about two and a half feet high. If he really was from W&D, he would have been considered in fair condition for his age. Next up was the old man. This was a little difficult because he was farther down, and I had to move some garbage around to get at him. His face was pinched into a mean grimace, and I wondered what kind of child would ever want to see something like this looking back at them from a Christmas window? No matter; I plunged ahead, tearing a few bags as I went, but I got him and wrestled him to the ground. He was a nasty-looking thing, but we stuffed him in the car. I kept thinking how I couldn't wait to spray these down with Lysol.

Last, but not least, came the dreaded reindeer. I climbed back on top of the station wagon and leaned into the dumpster. I knew that this would be hard—those other items were light, but this one was going to be a monster. It was starting to get dark, and I was really tired. I wished that Jim was with me to help, but he was out of town doing a magic show, and I was on my own, with only the young, cherubic face of a child staring up at me urging me on.

Heaving in a deep breath in and trying to hold it against the awful smell of garbage, I grabbed a hoof and pulled with all my might. My upper body was halfway in the dumpster. I had to exhale. It was awful. How do people make a living doing this? I grabbed again and pulled and pulled, and finally there was movement. I pulled again, and it started to move my way, but so did loose garbage, all coming toward me. I had to release my grip and take a step back. Another deep breath and in I went again. It went on like this for some time, but I finally managed to get the deer to the top of the dumpster. The thing was massive and seemed almost life-size. It was about five feet across from tail to nose and about four feet high. It must have weighed fifty to sixty pounds. When it landed on the roof of the station wagon, I thought it would leave a permanent dent.

I knew that I couldn't just throw it on the ground since it was so old and fragile, so I had to lower it to the ground. I don't know where I summoned the strength to do this, but it felt like the workout of a lifetime. With the car full of the other things, stuffing this deer into the backseat was not easy, but at least we could finally go home. All I could think about was a hot bath and clean pajamas.

Happily, we arrived safely home, and Jim was there. He unloaded the car and was amazed not only at our find but also that we had managed to get them all by ourselves. He put everything away in the garage, and we all went into the house and cleaned up. We all then ate a nice spaghetti dinner and rested. Later that night, after Erika went to bed, Jim and I decided to watch a 1960s concert on PBS. We were enjoying a nice Saturday evening when I decided I'd make some tea. I stood up to go into the kitchen and WHAM! "It" hit with a vengeance never before seen in either of our medical histories. Jim said, "Honey are you all right?" and WHAM! He was a goner, too.

And so began three days of the worst stomach flu imaginable, courtesy of the infamous W&D dumpster dive. Thankfully, Erika did not succumb. She never really did touch the items, so she was spared. Since the illness, the items were sanitized, and the smaller ones were occasionally brought to some of the talks that Jim and Erika have done around the area for libraries and service groups. We were never able to authenticate whether these items were ever really used at W&D or not, and because of that, we recently decided to dispose of the reindeer and his friends as well.

Santa Claus Is Coming to Town

Although the window displays drew people from as far away as fifty miles, which was a long distance to travel on winter roads back in 1937, G. Irving Latz wanted more. Latz's son, G. Irving Jr., put it this way: "Christmas got bigger every year and became a focal point of life in Fort Wayne." He was right, and W&D was the center of it all.

"We did all these things, and we did them well, but we didn't use religion to build our business. At the same time, we knew that it was important to support this part of Christmas," he continued. Wanting to give the community and W&D's patrons more every year, the giant lighted Santa Claus and Christmas wreath displays were introduced, and both started with small drawings. Not many know that the original sketch was a quick one done by Mr. Latz himself when the idea first came to him. Little did he know that he was creating a part of Fort Wayne history.

Enter Isabelle Wilkinson Parker, a commercial artist who, at one time, worked for a sign company in Fort Wayne. She took the sketch supplied by Latz and embellished it, coming up with the precursor to the sign that we now know. Parker was the person who added the blinking whip to Santa's hand to create a little visual interest. The original sign was made of plywood and had more than forty thousand lights. The Brinkman Sign Company constructed it and also installed the bulbs. It was rumored that this sign has more light bulbs than some of the great displays of New York and Chicago.

The Santa and the wreath made their debuts in 1937 at the corner of Calhoun and Washington. During the creation of both signs, the president of the Brinkman Sign Company, Mr. Frank Dunigan, recalled the scene that Christmas: "Every year, the signs would be repainted and washed. They would then be hauled up the sides of the buildings with pulleys from the roof."

From the beginning, there was a bit of controversy concerning the Santa sign. Mr. Dunigan insisted that there were four reindeer right from its creation, but the chief of window displays, Allen Bixby, claimed that the original had only three reindeer. Bixby said, "People often asked me where the fourth reindeer was." And because of that interest, an extra lighted deer was added the second year the sign was displayed.

When both signs made their debut, Washington Boulevard was a two-way street. Some years later, it became a one-way thoroughfare, and this time, when Santa made his yearly appearance, he was heading the wrong way down a one-way street! Bixby related, "It was commonplace for people to jokingly ask why Santa had lost his sense of direction!"

Ms. Parker always seemed to be somewhat surprised over the reactions the Santa sign received. She always considered it just part of her job and confided to a newspaper reporter that she didn't even go see it the first night the signs were lit. Little did she know the impact her designs would have on the hearts and minds of the thousands who equate the start of the Christmas season with the lighting of those displays.

On a final note, while researching this book, we received a mysterious phone call from a man who told us that the displays that hang downtown now are counterfeit. He maintained that a secret deal had been made to take the original signs out to a neighboring county, burn them and take pictures of the burning to prove they were destroyed. He said that the displays seen at Christmastime now are complete reproductions, with none of the original materials remaining.

While this type of conspiracy theory is fascinating to hear, if not a little bizarre, it really only reinforces one thing: people really, and I mean *really*, care about these displays. They are a big part of the heart and soul of the holiday season in Fort Wayne. It's much like the main character in Dr. Seuss's *How the Grinch Stole Christmas!* who discovers that maybe Christmas wasn't bought in a store. Maybe Christmas was just "a little bit more."

Whether the story we were told by this caller was true, it really doesn't matter. The importance of these displays lie in the emotions attached to them. To the people of Fort Wayne, these feelings mean a great, great deal.

THE WREATH

Christmas wouldn't be complete without a few words about the giant Christmas wreath that the city is still lucky enough to have in its possession today.

First displayed in 1937 on the side of the W&D building at Calhoun and Washington, this sign stood an incredible twenty-five feet high and held more than forty thousand lights on its plywood frame. Although it was retired to the dusty recesses of the L.S. Ayers warehouse after the sale of W&D took place, that wasn't the end of the story.

At one point, the Fort Wayne Parks Board president, Byron Novitsky, accepted an offer to display the wreath at the Fort Wayne children's zoo. Parks department workers inspected the wiring and framework and not only agreed that it was salvageable but also that it would make a great addition to the once popular "Christmas at the Zoo" attraction.

Interestingly enough, the parks department could have also obtained the Santa display but thought that it was too large and would be too cumbersome to assemble. So Santa was left in the dark a little longer while the wreath continued to shine each Christmas season.

There is one last piece of information worth noting. There were a few years when the Santa and the wreath did not shine off the sides of W&D at Christmastime. This was because during the war years, Fort Wayne was a manufacturer of materials used for warfare and was thought to be a target for enemy attack. During that time, we were told that the lights were not lit to reduce the chance of enemy planes spotting the city at night. Secondly, it was thought to be a small way Fort Wayne could conserve energy during the war.

WEE WILLIE WAND AND THE WAND SHOP

As the legend goes, Wee Willie WanD—or Wilhelm, as he was more formally known—was born in the fairy kingdom of Day-Before-Yesterday and was the son of a sugar plum fairy and a wood nymph prince. Unlike all of the other elves or fairies in the kingdom, little Wilhelm never sprouted his wings. This horrified the entire community to the point that they began to shun him.

Luckily for little Wilhelm, his wise old grandmother, who just happened to be the Queen of Day-Before-Yesterday, had a special magic wand in her attic that she dusted off and gave to her grandson. So the story goes, Wilhelm became known to all as Wee Willie WanD. Wee Willie used his wand to make the kind of magic that helped others, and it was widely agreed that he had the very best magic of all: the magic of love.

To the delight of local children, the story of how this little guy came to be was printed yearly in the Fort Wayne newspaper. It was first printed on November 13, 1949, complete with illustrations. The idea for such a mascot came from Chester Leopold, and with a little help from the artistic hand of Isabelle Parker of Santa display fame, Wee Willie WanD came to life at W&D.

According to what we were told by Bud and Bill Latz, the "WanD" portion of the name came about in the same way as the name for the store's toiletry line: "W" and "D," or, said quickly, "W" an' "D," which spells the word "wand" but also sounds like the store's name. From that also sprang WanDerland, the epitome of Christmas fantasy for children across the country.

This little doll, no more than four inches tall, had quite an auspicious beginning. After the idea was conceived, the services of a husband and wife team who worked out of their garage in California were called on to bring the elf to "doll hood." The couple eventually went on to establish the Mattel™ Company and create the world's most famous doll, Barbie™.

A beautifully preserved Wee Willie WanD doll complete with original box. *Courtesy of Sue Hackleman.*

Where Fort Wayne Shopped

Wee Willie sold for one dollar sometime from the late 1940s through the 1950s. He could be found donning the tops of decorated packages, on ladies coats, pinned to children's clothes and even as a tree decoration. We are not sure how many people still have a Wee Willie WanD doll hiding in their attic, but hold on to it if you do because they are a treasure. And think of it this way: you might be harboring Barbie's™ grandfather up there.

Although Wee Willie was the first doll ever created by the Mattel™ Company, the idea must have caught on. We learned of one other department store in California that hired the husband and wife team to make a doll for the store. We don't know the name of the store, but the little doll was called Jump Jump. We had a faded photo of Jump Jump, but the quality was not good enough to reproduce for this book.

Once the powers that be saw what a hit they had in Wee Willie, it was obvious that he could be of more use to the store. By the time the Santa Claus show found its way to the afternoon TV airwaves, it was thought that using Wee Willie WanD as the mascot would be a great way to get the little ones from their place in line to Santa's lap. This cute little elf was so friendly

Early Wee Willie WanD dolls had metal shoes. Later ones were made of plastic. *Courtesy of Sue Hackleman.*

and loveable that he (although it was usually always a girl in the costume) helped the children relax. In this way, they would not be as nervous by the time they got their turn on the fuzzy red velvet lap of Santa. Wee Willie WanD was the perfect addition to WanDerland. We spoke with a wonderful lady by the name of Cynda (Elder) Clark, who had the pleasure of playing Wee Willie and recalled those days fondly for us in the following interview.

JK: What years did you play the part of Wee Willie WanD at Wolf and Dessauer?

Cynda: Well, I just did it for one year. I think it was 1967, and I already worked there.

JK: What did you do there at that time?

C: I worked in the men's department as one of the sales clerks. Someone came up to me and asked if I would be interested. They said, "Why don't you go up and see if the costume will fit."

JK: Now, who approached you about that?

C: One of the managers did. I was pretty petite at the time. There was one pair of slippery-looking shoes. I tried the costume on and it fit. That was it! They decided I was going to do it that year. I had always been fascinated by this. My mother worked at the store in the junior department, and she also drove the train through WanDerland for the kids for several years. I love kids, and my mother was always a lover of children. She enjoyed doing it so much, and I loved watching her year after year. She got so much joy from it. The kids were always so excited. The decorations were always so beautiful. It really did look like a fairyland.

JK: How long was this done?

C: Thanksgiving through Christmas. The whole time Santa was there. The animated figures that they had there were wonderful. I just can't express how much I got from it, from seeing the kids.

JK: Did you do this all day?

C: Yes, I did it during the day shift. I came in later and stayed all afternoon into the evening 'til they closed.

JK: You put in a pretty long day then. Did you work with Phil Steigerwald?

C: Yes and what really got me was that I was one of the little kids who used to visit Phil, and now I was his helper. It brought back so many good memories. There isn't anything around like it anymore.

JK: No, there certainly isn't.

C: No. And the costume was just like the little Wee Willie WanD doll we all had. It had wild colors. The jacket was pink, and the shoes were like a slipper with curled up toes. Like a little pixie. You'd greet the kids when they came in, and they would giggle and smile.

JK: Did you receive any training for this?

C: Just to be part of the Santa Claus theme. They saw how I had worked with people. I was a people person, and I just kind of fell into it. They told me, "You will portray Wee Willie in part of Santa's World." They weren't real strict or hard.

JK: Were you on during the television show?

C: Yes, with Engineer John, but they didn't have a lot of me because the cameras were on Engineer John and Phil. I was busy greeting the kids when they were coming in.

JK: Who else was involved in the show at that time?

C: Engineer John, Phil and Miss Jane (Hersha). You had a lot of people around.

JK: How many kids do you think you saw in a day?

C: The kids were lined up for so long before it started. I couldn't even guess. Phil never said no to any of them. He took every child that came no matter how long it took. He was wonderful.

JK: Do you have any special memories of working with him?

C: Just that if anyone could truly be Santa, it was Phil. He was so wonderful with the children. He was marvelous with them. His mannerisms, his ways were great!

JK: Describe what it was like when the kids went up to see Santa.

C: Well, we had a little trail that would weave around like a maze. You could see the closer they came the more excited they got. Some would bring their list with them. They would talk on about their list, and their eyes were so focused on Phil.

JK: Was your job to help so they wouldn't be so nervous?

C: Yes, I would talk to them and try to put them at ease. They were even mesmerized by me! They were really in a world of make-believe. To them it was magical, and no other place to be. They were so cute; some were so timid. It really depended on their ages. Overall, though, the majority of them were anxious.

JK: Were you in the pictures they took with Santa too?

C: No, I wasn't. I was just a worker. I watched a lot of it and got as much pleasure out of it as the children.

JK: That's probably why they chose you. You mentioned earlier that your mom drove the train, right?

C: Yes, she did it for two or three years. It went under a tunnel. The kids loved it, and I know my mom made it fun for them.

JK: How did that work? Was it included on the way to Santa?

C: No. The train was separate. It was extra. There was a tunnel and tons of snow. It was really nice.

JK: How about one last thought about Christmas at Wolf and Dessauer?

Where Fort Wayne Shopped

C: Just that I wish those times could come back. I wish the children today could experience all that and have the feelings I had as a child and even as a grown-up having been part of all. I'll never forget it.

In a 1949 issue of the Wolf and Dessauer employee newsletter, we read of another gal who played Wee Willie WanD and who had a bit of a celebrity past. Her name was Gwen Wilson. Gwen had aspirations to be an actress and spent three years in California attending the famous Pasadena Playhouse. After that, she moved to Hollywood and did get cast in a few speaking roles in films produced by Republic, Paramount, Warner Bros. and MGM Studios.

During that time, Gwen became acquainted with such notable stars as Victor Mature, Mickey Rooney, Veronica Lake and Bob Preston. She also sang with a trio that did work for MGM. That led to a singing career in Chicago, where Gwen was featured at the Ambassador West, and later as a soloist with the Jimmy Stier Band.

Fort Wayne was next on her stop when she moved with husband, Bob. Gwen had two children and settled down from her exciting career to become our own famous elf.

Some might call it silly to get emotionally attached to a character or a doll, but young and old alike, the folks of Fort Wayne really did. Wee Willie WanD meant something special to everyone. Countless phone calls came in to us from many people who wanted to express how much their Wee Willie dolls meant to them. Most kept it either lovingly displayed in a place of prominence or carefully tucked away and only brought out for the holiday season. It became clear that this doll was a real treasure and a tangible link with their childhood.

No story was as touching as one we were told by a Fort Wayne woman whom we met while doing a talk on Wolf and Dessauer at a local club meeting. This woman had two very good friends who each had a Wee Willie WanD doll when they were young. Both had lost their doll somewhere between the transition of girlhood to woman. It bothered them both so much that they searched through antique stores and flea markets hoping to come across a doll. One of the ladies was lucky enough to locate one, and she ecstatically called her friend to tell her. The other woman was happy for her but continued on her own search with determination.

Eventually, in their older years, both women discovered that they had breast cancer and went through their chemotherapy and radiation treatments together. The woman with the doll recovered and eventually went into full remission. The prognosis for her friend was grim, unfortunately, and she was told to prepare for the worst.

Knowing that she was soon to lose her lifelong friend, the woman with the doll called her friend and said excitedly, "Guess what? I've found you Wee Willie WanD doll!" She then made plans to visit her friend and told her that she found the doll at a flea market in another town. She told this white lie because she knew that her friend would never accept the one she owned as a gift. The doll did mean a lot to her, but not as much as her friend did, so she kissed her on the forehead and laid the doll on her pillow. The sick woman squeezed her hand in thanks, and both sat there in silence for a while, just enjoying what they both knew would be one of the last times they would have together.

The friend died soon after that visit. At the funeral parlor, Wee Willie WanD was placed on the pillow just as her friend had done when she gave it to her. The woman's daughter relayed that it was her mother's last dying wish to have the doll with her as she passed into eternity, and she thanked her mother's friend for the sacrifice she made in the name of friendship.

So is it silly to love a doll, or is it really more of what that doll represents to us? Wee Willie WanD reminded these ladies of their carefree days as girls—a time when holidays were magical, best friends were forever and all our loved ones who have passed on seem to be with us once again.

WANDERLAND

Out of WanDerland grew the WanD shop. Now all of the parts of WanDerland that were so amazing to a little person were falling into place. Can you imagine a store of your own with everything just your own size, and your parents weren't even allowed inside?

The WanD shop was for kids, period. They could spend their allowance and shop for Christmas presents for their mom, dad and the rest of their family. The staff, usually dressed like elves, would wrap their package so the secret of what was inside could be kept until Christmas. Now if that isn't the stuff of Christmas memories, I don't know what is. And it all started with a little doll.

We have two Wee Willie WanD dolls, and because their little faces are hand-painted, it's fun to notice the small differences in expressions between them. You can also find other varied details, perhaps due to the years they were issued, such as plastic shoes versus metal shoes. We have heard from people who have held on to their dolls for years and wouldn't give them up for anything. Thanks go to W&D fan Sue Hackleman, who sent us the great pictures of her own Wee Willie WanD dolls, complete with original box.

THE TELEVISION SHOW

It's a sure bet that anyone growing up in Fort Wayne or the surrounding counties will remember rushing home from school, grabbing a snack and plopping down in front of the television set to tune into WKJG for their daily thirty-minute fix of the *Santa in WanDerland* show.

Speaking personally now, I remember running in after getting off the bus from Hamilton Elementary School and turning on the old black-and-white TV set. I couldn't wait to see what was going on that day and if any of my friends were going to be on the show. It didn't really matter that basically the same thing happened on every show. The kids would come in, sit on Santa's lap and ask for the top thing they wanted for Christmas (as well as a few "surprises"). It also didn't bother me at all when my two older brothers laughed at me for believing that the man I was watching really *was* Santa.

They would tell me that anytime now some kid was going to pull Santa's beard off, and then everyone would know it was all fake. I can remember even now, forty years later, thinking, "What if they're right? What if that really happens, and the whole thing turns out to be make-believe?" But then, I would watch the show a little longer. Santa's beard never did come off, and my fears would subside. It all proved what I'd known all along: Santa was real, the show was great and my brothers were knuckleheads.

Looking back now, it's a wonder that anyone cared enough to go to the trouble of making this show a possibility. Thank goodness they did, though, because this was a television tradition for northeast Indiana children. Each daily show was thirty minutes long and was done in color. That's pretty impressive when you realize that color cameras back in the 1950s were very large, cumbersome and expensive. They were actually so expensive that the TV station only owned one!

Undaunted, the crew diligently packed up, transported and set up all of the equipment five days a week in Wolf and Dessauer's WanDerland, where they would capture the delightful antics of Santa, played admirably by Phil Steigerwald; Miss Jane, better known as Jane Hersha; and sportscasting legend, the late Hilliard Gates, who passed away within the last five to ten years. John Siemer, who played "Engineer John" on TV33, also appeared on the show. After the show was taped, everything would have to be packed up again and brought back to the studio in time for the five o'clock news.

The regulars of the show did their jobs so well that Santa forged himself in our minds as real. He played his role with such relish, it appeared to the children that both he and they were the stars.

Anyone now aged fifty or older can remember themselves wishing for a moment or two to share their Christmas list on the lap of the "real" Santa. The idea of a private audience with the big guy was better than waiting for the Sea Monkeys you ordered from the back of the comic book to arrive in the mail!

The other reason we all watched the show was to find out what all the new toys that year were going to be. If the kids on Santa's lap were all asking for the same thing, then you knew that toy had to be good! Any regular viewer of *Santa in WanDerland* also watched *The Uncle Wynn Show*. If you didn't know, Uncle Wynn was one of TV's first infomercials right here in Fort Wayne. Each evening, Uncle Wynn would come on television for five minutes and would demonstrate the latest and greatest toys that could all be found at Koehlingers Bicycle and Toy Store. Each broadcast, Uncle Wynn paraded the toys for the camera, one by one, and demonstrated what they did or described what you did with them.

One toy that stands out in my memory was Fu Chu. Fu Chu was a plastic cup that held about fifty strips of bamboo, each with a number from one to fifty stamped on it. The idea was to gently shake the cup up and down until one bamboo stick worked its way out from the others and fell to the floor. You would then look at the number on the stick and read the corresponding fortune in the booklet that came with it. Although Fu Chu was hardly scientific, it was at least as accurate as any television weather forecast.

Another of my favorites was a game called Fang Bang, in which four players donned cardboard masks and held a balloon with a plastic snakehead attached to it. The snake heads each had a sharp pointy tongue and the heads were attached to the balloons with rubber bands. At the signal, the players would duel with their "snakes" until their opponent's balloon popped and one person was declared the winner. Something tells me that in this age of political correctness, this toy wouldn't be the big seller it was back then, but is seems like childhood was more fun when I was a kid.

Can you remember when Santa—who was worried about Rudolph's chicken pox and whether or not he would recover in time to lead the team on Christmas Eve—instructed every child watching to cross their fingers and to keep them that way until Christmas? What a job teachers across the viewing area had trying to get kids to uncross those fingers so they could hold their pencils!

How about Santa's catchphrase on the show, "No peeking!" Nostalgic memories are kind of bittersweet. It's fun to recall, with longing, those simple times that were indeed magical to us. I find myself wishing that I could somehow create that same feeling for my own kids. Christmas just doesn't feel the same anymore. Maybe I'm just older, but now whatever the secret ingredient that stirs up that feeling is, W&D had it and sprinkled it pretty liberally throughout Fort Wayne.

Christmas at Wolf and Dessauer, and all that went with it, reminds me of the song "Puff the Magic Dragon." In that song, Puff sadly slips off into his cave and is never seen again because Jackie Paper no longer needs him. Children grow, times change and technology takes over, but we still need those memories. I still think that I'm lucky to have raised my children where people cared enough to do things like restore a Santa sign and make a yearly event out of it. It makes me happy to hear people talk about what the downtown area used to be like and what an occasion shopping at W&D was. I appreciate the fact that the Embassy Center is now creating its own Christmas window displays every year and that the history center has its own displays as well.

Because Fort Wayne is a community that cares about its past, we can all embrace our memories of W&D. From its very beginning, from all of the people who worked there and every story they can share, each adds a piece to what made this place tick. W&D has remained in the heart of this city for one hundred years, and I have a feeling that it will remain there well into the future.

How Much Is that Polar Bear in the Window?

One name that kept coming up continually in all conversations with the people we interviewed was Walter Tharp. Walter was the display director for Wolf and Dessauer for more than thirty years. Under the direction of his boss, Chester Leopold, Walter's artistic hand was responsible for most of the wonderful things we remember. Once it was decided what wonders would be created any given year, Tharp was most likely the artist who brought it all to life.

In 1946, Walter was a student at Central High School, where he was enrolled in a vocational art program. Part of the program was on-the-job training that earned you high school credit while working where the school placed you. Walter was lucky enough to wind up at Wolf and Dessauer. He remained in this program until graduation and was then hired as a full-time employee.

Walter's early jobs included making signs by hand and by machine and then advancing to window displays and store decorations. Within a few years, Walter's talent was evident, and he was promoted to display director. Along with that title came enormous responsibilities.

We met Walter for breakfast at the Renaissance Restaurant near South Town Mall on a Friday morning. He is a quiet, affable man whom we instantly liked. Over coffee, he shared with us a thick portfolio of original drawings, photographs, slides and tons of information that we would otherwise never have known. Some of those creations we've shared in this book with you.

Although his artistic influence was apparent in so much of what we saw, he was slow to take any credit for himself. Instead, he simply replied, "I had a great team." Unlike most stores today, Wolf and Dessauer had an entire fleet of carpenters, painters, drapery makers and electricians to create whatever the staff could dream up. To name a few, Walter's team included Darrel Monroe, Nadyne Carr and Miles Bryant. It was interesting that after all these years, Walter recalled these names as if he had just seen these old friends yesterday.

Since Walter worked closely with Chester Leopold, who was the public relations and advertising manager, we asked Walter to tell us his opinion of his boss. Walter said, "He was great to work for. He believed in his people, and

Design ideas drawn up by Walter Tharp. *Authors' collection.*

More of Walter's ideas in the planning stages. *Authors' collection.*

he was a perfectionist. He treated you with respect, and that made us all want to do a good job...We had a good time going to shows and planning. Chester was constantly ahead of the game. He could talk Bud Latz into anything!"

The shows he was referring to were the yearly trade shows where the display houses would show off their new products for store decoration and design. It was always the first week of July and would alternate each year between Chicago and New York. Every year, Walter and Mr. Leopold would pick out what they thought would be the most exciting ways to decorate the windows and interior of the stores.

After our lengthy quest to find genuine W&D window figures, we were thrilled to hear the real scoop from Walter. The company that produced most of the animated figures for those famous W&D windows was Sylvestri Arts, located in Chicago. Walter recalled his favorite windows: "After all of these years, I can still tell you the phone number and address of Sylvestri's." Another bit of trivia about the windows was the fact that there was indeed a second company from which "mini-window animations" were purchased. That company was David Hamburger's in New York, but its products weren't quite the same caliber as Sylvestri's, and W&D only bought from it occasionally.

Since the Christmas windows were such a big part of Wolf and Dessauer's holiday magic, we had a lot of questions about them, and Walter was more than happy to fill us in. We asked how much a typical holiday window would cost. When Walter told us the average cost was between $15,000 and $20,000 for one large window, we were astounded. Keep in mind that those were the figures in the 1950s and 1960s—this would have been an absolute fortune. According to Walter, the Latz family thought that it was justified because thousands of people would be there when the windows were unveiled. It was the reason people came to the store in the first place during the holiday season.

In this day and age, it would be a rare thing for a company to look at anything other than its profit margin. Spending that amount of money today without a guarantee of return would be unheard of. To Wolf and Dessauer, however, this was an important tradition, and here we see some insight into just one of the reasons people still reminisce about the store.

We asked Walter how he knew whether or not his creations were successfully received. He replied, "I would browse around in the crowd listening to people's expressions and what they said. When I heard the children 'ooh' and 'ahh,' then I knew it was good." Hearing that reply, we wanted to know if he ever had a favorite window of his own. Walter couldn't pick out a particular favorite but thought they were all good. He said their focus was to keep outdoing themselves year after year. He enjoyed the challenge, and it motivated him.

This was all so incredible to us; we had never realized what a behind-the-scenes operation was involved in the running of Wolf and Dessauer. That's why when it came to the windows, no detail was spared. Walter told us that whenever something like a puff of smoke or fog was needed for a baking scene or a potbellied stove, dry ice was used. Of course, this meant that somebody had to keep replenishing the supply. That duty usually fell to Walter. He told us, "When the store was closed on a Sunday, people would still go downtown to see the windows, so I would have to go down there three or four times a day. I had my own key. My kids would love it because we had the whole store to ourselves, and it was a big deal to them."

Eventually, the conversation got around to WanDerland, and we discovered that under the direction of Chet Leopold, Walter's designs helped bring it to life. "I drew the sketches and then would get Chet's input. We'd just do it," He said.

Any child who sat on Santa's lap must have marveled at the immense throne Santa occupied. During our discussion, we found out Walter designed that as well and then sent the plans to the carpenter.

Where Fort Wayne Shopped

You might wonder at the title of this section. We wanted to know if Walter could remember any funny incident or any windows that didn't turn out just right. At first he couldn't think of any, but then a smile crossed his face and he relayed this story:

> *I remember one. I got it my head that we just had to have a polar bear for one of the window scenes. It just so happened that a member of the team, Nadyne Carr, and her husband used to eat at a restaurant in Marion that had a stuffed polar bear in the lobby. She found out that it came from a gravel company south of Indianapolis named "Driver's Concrete and Gravel." I called them, and they told me that they had one, and I could run right down and pick it up, so I made arrangements to get a store truck and got ready to go. Now, I figured this bear would be about the size of a man, so I was expecting big, but when I saw it, was I ever shocked! This thing must have been twelve feet tall, and it had its mouth open, with its teeth bared and all of its claws out! I thought to myself, "Oh Lord what have I gotten myself into!"*
>
> *Well, the owner of the company was a hunter that went on expeditions every year, and this bear was one he actually shot and had stuffed. I couldn't back out now, so I loaded it up in the truck and headed back to Fort Wayne. When I got there, I realized this thing was so big it wouldn't even fit in a window, so I had to figure out what I was going to do with it. Eventually, I decided to put a bow around its neck and a giant candy cane in one arm. We mounted a mannequin on a turntable and put one hand up so that when it turned it appeared to be dancing with the bear. Even then, it still looked so ferocious I thought it would scare the kids to death, but when I saw one of them looking a little hesitant, I would just tell them, "Oh no kids, don't be scared he's not growling, he's just smiling at you." They bought it. I don't know why that one worked but it did.*

We walked away from this interview with Walter just feeling happy. He was such a warm and engaging man that it's really no surprise that most of your fond Christmas memories began with him. After Walter retired, he still continued with his art and showed us photographs of two eight-foot-tall murals that he had painted. One was a depiction of Christ and the other his interpretation of Ezekiel 1:10.

Sadly, Walter passed away on January 2, 2011, and with him went one of the last physical links to our connection with the ghosts of Christmases long gone by. Our condolences go out to Walter's family. He was a wonderful man.

Let's Go Shopping

A Pet Department?

Many people say that they wish they could close their eyes, turn back the hands of time and be standing in front of Wolf and Dessauer, dressed in their finest and ready to walk in those doors for a day of fun and memories.

Full-service store that it was, it's truly amazing to think of the range of products and services that was available at Wolf and Dessauer. If you are in your fifties or older, you will remember that most department stores had pet departments. Remember those turtles that we all used to have? Wolf and Dessauer didn't have a pet department, did it?

Bird cages with birds adorning the store.
Courtesy of Walter Tharp.

Not only did it have a pet department, it had quite an exotic one at that. From the 1950s through the early 1960s, having songbirds on display to signal the beginning of spring became a tradition at Wolf and Dessauer. Also on hand were dark canaries, which were the result of crossbreeding canaries and European finches.

At that time, the manager of the pet department imported the birds from Holland. They traveled, in one day, from Holland to New York and arrived in Fort Wayne the following day. The birds were displayed inside a bird cage that was placed inside a large white wicker basket. It was then suspended from the ceiling and filled with dozens of flowers, greenery and green tulle. Oddly enough, it wasn't the responsibility of the pet department to maintain the birds. That job fell to the display department, under the direction of Walter Tharp.

A TOUCH OF THE GOOD LIFE

From the very beginning, Wolf and Dessauer did everything wholeheartedly for the pleasure of its customers. To make the customer feel special was the mission. It brought Fort Wayne the first signs of the changing seasons, taught us how to entertain with style, dress with class and accessorize perfectly. Wolf and Dessauer showed us how to cook for dinner parties, decorate our homes and wrap the perfect gift. Just like sitting down with a good romance novel, Wolf and Dessauer gave us the opportunity to see bits and pieces of the world that we never would have had the chance to see on our Fort Wayne, middle-class incomes. It brought the entire world to our fingertips, literally. In the glove department alone, there was merchandise from five different European and Far East countries represented.

Wolf and Dessauer carried jewelry from Siam (now Thailand), clocks from Germany and lingerie from France and the Philippines. One could shop for shoes and sandals not only from Italy but also from Ireland and Switzerland, as well as the finest sweaters from England and China.

The crystal and glassware departments were the only place in Fort Wayne that carried Baccarat crystal from France, which had been known as the "crystal of the Kings" since 1765. There was antique silver for sale that dated back to 1870. There was also Dansk woodenware from Scandinavia that was made from rare woods from the jungles of Nicaragua, Brazil and east Africa.

The Gourmet Shop was a paradise for food lovers and had selections from more than twelve different countries, including chutney from India and

Left: The store, decked out for the holidays. *Courtesy of Walter Tharp.*

Below: Holiday merchandise ready for purchase. *Courtesy of Walter Tharp.*

shortbread from Scotland. There was also a candy shop featuring all kinds of delicious treats for young and old alike. It was evident that the good taste and purchasing skills of the store's buyers truly made Wolf and Dessauer a beautiful place to spend many hours shopping. Each department was a feast for the senses, and the people of Fort Wayne remember it all.

THE STORE MODELS

Often, when we ask people about what they remember most about Wolf and Dessauer, we hear about the famous models. We've been told that the models were beautiful, graceful and elegant ladies, and we've heard that they were kept very busy. Their job was to wear the latest fashions and walk through the store to show the customers what was available and how it should be worn. They also had to be available for photo shoots for store advertising and for newspaper ads.

When Wolf and Dessauer would plan a special sale or promotion, it would often use the models in different scenes that were built around promoting a specific idea. For instance, when it was decided to host a store-wide showcase

A newspaper ad featuring summer fashions. *Authors' collection.*

based on Kay Corinth's and Mary Sargeant's book *All About Entertaining*, a book that was first released at Wolf and Dessauer, it did it up big time. Along with creating scene-stealing windows, the design department transformed the third floor, from escalator to tearoom, into four vignettes ranging from a bachelor party to a fiftieth wedding anniversary dinner. On the second floor, they showcased a glamorous buffet, as well as an afternoon tea and a fun beach party.

The auditorium on the fourth floor featured a collection of invitations and party preparations. There were guest speakers on every subject and even five more vignettes featuring dining on the patio, a child's birthday gala, family room fun and an informal brunch where the public enjoyed coffee after the show. The Wolf and Dessauer models brought everything to life through demonstrations and their graceful presence in every scene. True to form, no expense was spared in making a success out of this event.

Then there were the fashion shows. Almost every season, the models went to work under the guidance of Barbara Hutmacher, who was the fashion coordinator for the 1960s shows. The spring, fall and back-to-school events were the largest. To add to the amount of work, there was always a college show that took place in the auditorium for girls wondering what college would be like and what kind of clothes they would need to fit the part.

The women's foundation department. *Courtesy of Ken Lucas.*

Where Fort Wayne Shopped

Wolf and Dessauer even sponsored fashion shows just for its co-workers so the employees would see exactly what the customer saw on the runway. The shows were elegant, precisely timed and very dramatic.

In addition to the seasonal shows, there were holiday shows, shows only for accessories, lingerie shows and even shows only featuring shoes. Barbara Hutmacher had a very busy job, being responsible for most of the wonderful fashion show memories that people still remember.

Some Wolf and Dessauer models during the 1960s were Alleda Elam, Gladys Swift, Ethel Merryman, Helen Pyles, Harriet Lynch, Rose Mary Woods, Jull Smith, La Von Geis and Doris Clark Bogner.

After a quick look at the clothing carried in various departments and how important fashion was at Wolf and Dessauer, we thought we'd highlight an article that was included in the *Co-Worker*, the W&D employee newsletter:

LET'S VISIT 7TH AVENUE
Written by Eleanor Stoner
Fashion Coordinator, W&D, June 1947

In just a handful of skyscrapers within a few blocks of each other is concentrated the wholesale ready-to-wear industry. This section, although somewhat unattractive to view, houses one of the most colorful and fascinating of industries. Hurrying down the street during "season" we are shoved back and forth by the mobs of garment workers who mill aimlessly around—especially before 9:00 and at lunch time. Numerous pushcarts and hand trucks add to the confusion.

After a brief trip by elevator up through one of these mammoth structures, we finally emerge completely breathless from the melee.

Glancing around, we find ourselves in a showroom which is a perfect setting for displaying the latest fashions. Often, bolts of bizarre fabrics are strewn around to create atmosphere. Models with a regal air show the fashions which have taken several months to ready for this tremendous influx of buyers. Some fashions will be adaptations of Parisians imports, names familiar to most, Lucien Lelong, Balenciaga, Christian Dior, Molyneus, Pierre Mlamain, Gres.

Behind the scenes, we find designers stroking a rabbit's foot for luck or pampering some equally foolish superstition connected with opening days. A second glance shows us that the designer is still biased, for he almost always insists on completely accessorizing the models as they prepare to show the line.

This line very often consists of from one hundred to two hundred pieces, several of which will later be discarded as "dogs" never to be cut or delivered to the customer.

The season lasts only a few weeks. Then designers once more begin the arduous task of selecting new fabrics and trimmings, styling the line, fitting the models, and shaping up a new collection for next season. Poor production man! His headaches are just beginning!

Here is another interesting fashion article:

SKETCHING A NEW FASHION PICTURE…W&D STYLE
Written by Eleanor Stoner
Fashion Coordinator, W&D, July 1947

After being regimented during the war years, we now face a season where there is a complete change in fashion. It is typified by the "figure eight" silhouette consisting of narrower and rounder shoulders, rounded padded hiplines and skirts that are longer, approximately fourteen inches off the floor, although this is an individual problem depending on height and figure.

It is important to balance such a silhouette; so we have a change in accessories:

Hats: with side-to-side width and crowns that are deeper and fuller.

Bags: larger and deeper but with softer styling for longer skirts.

Gloves: longer with above-the-wrist interest to blend with the tapering sleeve and rounder shoulders, Gauntlets, flares, turn-back cuffs and tailored types are particularly fine.

Jewelry: necklaces are very important and fill in the uncluttered bodice. They denote the feeling of downward motion and keep pace with the over-all lengthening of the silhouette. Earrings are larger and tend to balance the side-to-side look in hats with contour styles, clusters and loops. Bracelets are smart with the new understated sleeve. They are larger and wider. Flexible chains banded cuffs and tailored types are particularly fine.

Hosiery: is now more than ever a real fashion accessory. Darker and more sheer, blending into an unbroken line from head to foot which ties in with the longer skirt and higher shoes.

Shoes: with a higher, more closed look, styled with delicacy and exquisite detail. Draping cutwork, piping and restrained trims are prominent.

It might also be wise to start looking for longer slips and foundations that nip in the waistline.

THE AUTOMOTIVE STORE

With all of the time we put into research and talking to folks about their memories, there were times when we thought that we knew everything there was to know about Wolf and Dessauer. It was then we would hear things that completely surprised us! That's how we felt when we discovered, and verified with Bud and Bill Latz, that Wolf and Dessauer even had an automotive store. When a friend of ours wanted to buy an antique Goodyear tire stand for her son as a gift, we stumbled across an old photo. We didn't think anything of it until we looked a little harder and saw that the writing on the windows of the business was reflected in a mirror behind the counter. Sure enough, it read "Wolf and Dessauer Automotive Store."

The place was clean as a whistle, unlike so many of the grimy garages you would have found during that same period of time. According to the Latz brothers, the store was around in the 1920s and 1930s and did a thriving business.

THE GARDEN DEPARTMENT

We were surprised again to learn that there was also a garden department located on Berry Street, and it carried just about anything anyone could want for their gardens. It included ornamental trees, tulips, roses, willows, maples and birch trees. There was a greenhouse with shrubs, and even Lawnboy and Toro mowers and tractors were sold.

When we picture Wolf and Dessauer, we never thought of it as having gardens covered, too. It was much like the Lowe's and Home Depot stores of today, except that it was about fifty years ahead of its time.

THE CREDIT UNION

The Wolf and Dessauer co-workers Federal Credit Union was organized in 1936 for the twofold purpose of encouraging savings among the employees and to make loans to its members. Interest on loans was 0.75 percent on the unpaid balance.

One could join the credit union by applying to Carl Schaffer, who was the treasurer. The credit union was housed on the fifth floor, and the membership fee was only twenty-five cents. You could deposit as little or as much as you wanted, but when a co-worker saved five dollars, they were considered a stockholder and received dividend shares, which were declared at the annual stockholders' meeting.

The Warehouses

The Washington Street warehouse was the beating heart of Wolf and Dessauer, and only an insider would know all of the things that went on behind those closed doors.

Every day, all of the operations that were essential to the existence of Wolf and Dessauer were completed in both the Washington and Columbia Street warehouses. The one on Washington was established in 1947 and continued to grow through the years. The processing of all merchandise was carried out there, and so were all the functions of shipping and city delivery.

All incoming merchandise for the store was unloaded at the Washington warehouse docks and then placed on the receiving platform. Receiving reports were filled out and attached to the merchandise. Another man would load the merchandise on a large conveyor belt, which then transported it to the second floor. Once there, it was opened, carefully checked, listed, marked with prices and then sent to the appropriate department.

With the constant arrival of thousands of new items every day, there wasn't always room available at the main store, and so they were moved to the basement stockrooms. The Wolf and Dessauer stockrooms were known in the retail industry for being well organized and immaculate. When individual buyers requested their merchandise, it would sometimes be sent to them directly from there.

It was the Washington Street warehouse that handled all of the outgoing mail. When packages for out-of-town customers were brought from the main store to the shipping department, the contents of each package were checked against the sales ticket to be sure that everything was there and in good condition. The merchandise was then repackaged, wrapped and sent out by either parcel post, express or freight, whichever would prove to be the quickest and most efficient. Claims and returns to manufacturers were handled here as well.

DISPENSARY

Because of the large number of employees, Wolf and Dessauer maintained its own dispensary where co-workers who were feeling ill could utilize the services of the store's own registered nurse. Insurance and hospitalization records were kept there as well.

AMY LEE

The Amy Lee department was a personal shopping service for customers who needed assistance in choosing gifts for others or even items for themselves. The Amy Lee girls provided their services for out-of-town customers and also to those who were unable to get away from their daily routines to shop on their own. These ladies took their jobs very seriously and did their best to also help businessmen, husbands and other busy people find just the right gift to give a caring touch of class. Some of those very helpful Amy Lee co-workers included Catherine Pandorff, director of the Amy Lee Shopping Service; Margaret Weber; Irene Abt; Joan Cartwright; Betty Wietfield; Pat Perry; and Mary Shields.

Here is a letter written by an Amy Lee customer that we found fun to read. It was taken from the July 19, 1947 issue of the *Co-Worker*.

> *Hello Amy Lee,*
>
> *This is a customer calling. I want to thank you for the sympathetic and courteous service the Amy Lee girls have always extended to me and my family. We live on a small farm and are not always able to get into town to shop. However, that has been no problem since we discovered that a word to you will bring us merchandise selected just as carefully as anything we ourselves might purchase. We especially appreciate the dispatch with which you've handled our exchanges. Last Christmas, you even shopped with my harried husband. Thanks, Amy Lee!*

FINE DINING AT WOLF AND DESSAUER

One of the things that *everyone* remembers about Wolf and Dessauer is the delicious food they enjoyed there. Wolf and Dessauer had quite a number of eating establishments that ranged from the employee-only cafeteria and the sandwich counter to the elegant tearoom where celebrations were held and special memories were made. There was also the ever-fashionable Le Baton restaurant, which was modeled after a French café. It didn't really matter where you chose to eat, when you were hungry at Wolf and Dessauer you could always find something to suit your taste.

Le Baton was originally a coffeehouse adapted from the French version of the open-air café. It was so popular that it quickly evolved as Fort Wayne's most unique eating establishment, a place where patrons would enjoy a complete luncheon, dessert or even an elegant supper. Le Baton was decorated with big coach lamps and striped, green-and-white awnings. There were beautiful marble-topped tables and wrought-iron chairs. Hanging throughout the café were baskets of live greenery and old-fashioned white ceiling fans.

Le Baton brought a little bit of Paris to Fort Wayne, with handsome waiters attired in the French garçon style, dispensing not only exemplary service but also many epicurean delights. If Le Baton were still here, it would no doubt still be a favorite gathering place.

We were unable to verify this, but if you like celebrity gossip, word has it that both Marilyn Monroe and Bob Hope visited La Baton on separate occasions when their business brought them through Fort Wayne.

Another favorite spot mentioned by almost every person we spoke to was the Wolf and Dessauer tearoom. It truly was a place where memories were made. The linens were crisp and perfect, and the sumptuous dishes were sometimes decorated with origami-like swans just to make the occasion a little more special.

The tearoom is where the store held its important functions, such as retirement lunches and special meetings. It is also where visiting executives were treated to some special elegance. On some occasions, a four o'clock tea was served to commemorate extra-special events.

Wolf & Dessauer
FOUNTAIN CHECK

CLERK / GUEST

Soup

Salad

Sandwich

Dessert

Beverage

Coco Cola

Fountain

PLEASE
Pay Cashier
Thank You

A guest check from the W&D fountain.
Authors' collection.

Vinegar and Oil Dressing

1 pt Salad oil

1½ pt Vinegar

3 Cups Sugar

4 Tablespoons Salt

2 " " White Pepper

1 large grated Onion

1 Cup Chopped Peppers

1 cup " Pimento

mix and let stand over night

DAILY SUGGESTIONS

All foods served at the fountain prepared in our
Sixth Floor Daylight Kitchen

All glassware and chinaware thoroughly sterilized.

Wednesday	November 24, 1937

LUNCHEON MENU

Fresh Vegetable Soup............10¢
Corn Chowder...................,..10¢
Diced Fruit Cup...............10¢

Luncheon #1.
Baked Virginia Ham – Sweet Potatoes, Green
Beans, Rolls & Butter, Coffee.........30¢

Luncheon #2.
Creamed Chicken Giblet in Noodle Nest –
Cranberry Sauce, Rolls & Butter........25¢

HOLIDAY SPECIAL
Hot Sliced Turkey Sandwich, Molded
Cranberry Salad, Coffee...............35¢

ADDED SELECTIONS
Soup, Baked Ham Sandwich & Coffee......25¢

Cottage Cheese on Pineapple Ring, French
Dressing, Saltines....................20¢

SANDWICHES
Minced Beef.........10¢ Peanut & Bacon..15¢
Ham Salad..........15¢ Chopped Egg.....15¢

SALADS
Potato Salad........10¢ Ham Salad.......15¢
Fruit Salad.........10¢ Egg Salad.......15¢

DESSERTS
Fresh Apple, Apricot Cream or Cherry Pie
....10¢
Homemade Cake.......10¢ Lemon Sherbet...10¢
Hot Chocolate, Wafers.......10¢

Luncheon Menu Changed Daily

Above: The handwritten ingredients for W&D's vinegar and oil dressing. *Authors' collection.*

Right: The fountain menu of the day. *Authors' collection.*

Another great eatery that did a booming lunch trade was the soda fountain. We received a lovely note from a very sweet lady who worked there. We called her up and decided to include our interview with Maxine Rudrow here.

JK: Hi Maxine. What years did you work at Wolf and Dessauer?

Maxine: I worked there eight years. I stopped in 1956. I was pregnant. I went back later and worked there about seven more years at the new store.

JK: Where was the new store? Do you mean after the fire?

M: No. This was later on when they built across from the Hobby House.

JK: What did you do there?

M: I did a little bit of everything. When I started out, I never had worked a day in my life. Someone told me that if I was going to work at Wolf and Dessauer that I should go to the fountain because it was so nice. She had worked there and said you didn't have to pay out a lot of money for special clothing or meals like that and that you made more money.

The men's shoe department. *Photo by Ken Lucas.*

A display outside the smoke shop. *Photo by Ken Lucas.*

The men's department. Notice the Purdue shirt on display. *Courtesy of Ken Lucas.*

JK: I assume that, for a first job, that sounded pretty good to you?

M: Yes, and I started out as a waitress in the soda fountain. See, we had a soda fountain that was very popular. We seated ninety-four people at a time.

JK: Did you have a full house every day?

M: Oh yes. We would start serving around eleven o'clock and it took two co-workers working as fast as they could just to keep up on sandwiches. And of course our pies and soups came from the tearoom.

JK: Was everything made at the store?

M: Oh yes. We made wonderful ham salad. You couldn't beat it, it was so popular. Then I would make salad and work the sandwich board. When I left they had offered me the manager's job. I did that for a few months but then I had to leave.

JK: To have your baby?

M: Yes. I wasn't expecting that because I already had one child, and there was nineteen years between them.

JK: That's quite a number of years.

M: Well, it was quite a shock, and I really hated to leave.

JK: Do you have any special memories of events that happened while you were working there?

M: I don't know. They were all special. We were so busy. We made a lot of salad! I just liked it a lot!

JK: I can understand that. Now, what else did you serve there? Did you make that red velvet cake I'm always hearing about?

M: No. We didn't do that. We had the pies and the soda fountain. We made our own chocolate syrup, you know, because it was special. I think I mentioned a drink we made that was very popular in the hot weather.

Right: A view of the photo department. *Courtesy of Ken Lucas.*

Below: The Kodak camera counter. *Courtesy of Ken Lucas.*

Photography classes were held here. *Courtesy of Ken Lucas.*

JK: Which one was that?

M: The Orange Freeze. It was very simple but people loved it. You took a glass, put two dips of orange sherbet in it and poured orange juice over it. That was it and they loved it.

JK: Maxine, did you ever take part in making any of the other food yourself?

M: At one time.

JK: What did you make?

M: Well, I made the frozen salad and just different things like that.

JK: Do you remember the names of any of your co-workers?

M: There was Irene Getz, Martha Winters, Eve Sanderson, Betty Pecker and that's the most that I worked with. They were a little older and worked behind the counter.

Where Fort Wayne Shopped

JK: What did you like most about working at Wolf and Dessauer?

M: Oh, I guess it was my first job, and I just fell in love with it. I loved being around food. That was one thing I did know!

JK: I'm reading the card you sent us. It says you served the famous Wolf and Dessauer cashew butter, right?

M: Yes, that was very popular. You don't see that around too much anymore today.

JK: It was like peanut butter, just with cashews?

M: Yes, only one store in town sold it. I don't know where we got ours, but there used to be a little store on Creighton that sold it, but of course that's gone long ago.

JK: Did you buy your clothes and get special deals because you worked there?

M: Yes. And I can remember one time being on the elevator with Bud Latz. We were going up, and they had just started carrying petite sizes for women, and of course that made me happy because I'm not very large. I was telling him how nice that was. And we also had an elevator person that ran the elevator. I always thought that was so nice because I still don't like elevators.

JK: What other jobs did you do? Did you ever sell clothing?

M: No, I stayed in the fountain. When they opened the Huntington store, they asked me to go there. I didn't want to go. Then at one time, I can't remember too much about it, but Wolf and Dessauer served food at the airport, too.

JK: Really? How many years did they do that?

M: I don't know how long they did it or anything like that because I wasn't involved with it, but I do know they served food there for time. It didn't last very long, though.

Above: French foundations trunk showing. *Courtesy of Ken Lucas.*

Left: One of Wolf and Dessauer's live French lingerie shows. *Courtesy of Ken Lucas.*

Where Fort Wayne Shopped

Modeling French fashions. *Photo by Ken Lucas.*

JK: Wow. That is really interesting. I've never heard that before.

M: And on the second floor, they had a very nice cafeteria just for the co-workers. But the fountain was bigger.

JK: I suppose lunchtime was the busiest time of day?

M: Oh yes, it was so busy. People just stood behind the chairs, and as soon as they were empty, someone new would just jump right in. We had busboys. It was all very nice.

JK: Was working in other store departments just as nice?

M: I think it was from what I've heard.

JK: Maxine, I ask everyone who ever worked there this same question. Why do you think the customers loved Wolf and Dessauer so much and remember it so fondly even today?

M: Oh, I don't know. It was just so nice, and people were so nice to the customers. I know my mother lived in Michigan, and she just loved to come down and shop at Wolf and Dessauer.

JK: Is there anything else you'd like to say about your time there?

M: I just loved it. I think all of the co-workers had a bond with the store. Some had been there a lot longer than I had, and it seemed like when they moved over to the other store, it was never the same. The fountain was put in the basement and they added a grill, but it was never the same.

JK: Well Maxine, it has been a pleasure, and you gave me a lot of insight. Thanks for your time and thanks for all of your memories.

Fashions shown on a mannequin. *Courtesy of Ken Lucas.*

Fashions shown on a live model, complete with co-workers. *Courtesy of Ken Lucas.*

An area set aside for fashion shows. *Courtesy of Ken Lucas.*

Here are two interesting pieces that came from the Wolf and Dessauer employee newsletter, the *Co-Worker*, December 1949 issue. They fit perfectly here:

Salute to a Fountain Girl, Gertrude Sweet

There are many co-workers who cannot be grouped in a sales category; and yet in a larger sense, these individuals are selling W&D and its policies just as surely as the salespeople themselves. Since this is especially true of the girls in the Fountain, we have selected Gertrude Sweet for this issue's Salute to a Sales Person.

Actually, when it comes to job qualification and performance, there is little difference between Gertrude and a selling co-worker. Personal appearance is, in both instances of primary importance. By the same token, whether a customer is considering a chocolate soda or a fur coat, prompt approach, courtesy and the best possible service are essential.

"We even use suggestive selling" Gertrude told us. "For instance, 'How about a salad with your sandwich,'" or "'The pie is very *good today.'"*

Experience has taught Gertrude that a job is always a selling proposition, no matter what her duties may be.

The W&D Employee Cafeteria

Why have prices in the Co-Workers Cafeteria been increased, and why have certain items been taken off the menu?

When the Co-Worker's Cafeteria was first instituted, Wolf and Dessauer felt that this operation should not be allowed to make a profit. Through the month of October of this year, the Cafeteria showed a loss of $16,951; through the same period last year, this loss was $14,230. From the above figures it is obvious that the Co-Workers Cafeteria is not operating as it was originally intended for it is showing a loss of about $2000 a month. In order to reduce this figure, two things were done.

Certain items were eliminated from the menu. They were main courses which would have required a 50% to 100% price increase to cover the cost of preparation. We felt this would be too great of a price change. Some item prices were increased a few cents, just enough to cover the cost of preparation.

Above: Departments were always busy during the live fashion shows. *Courtesy of Ken Lucas.*

Right: A not-so-typical window display. *Courtesy of Ken Lucas.*

And here is one more humorous item found associated with the tearoom. Apparently, there were no disposable aluminum or tin pie pans at the time, so when an employee bought a pie and brought it home, they brought the tin home as well and very often neglected to bring it back (from the 1948 *Co-Worker*):

> *Our pastry cooks will be baking those dee-licious Tea Room pies in crocks if some of you pie fanciers don't start returning their pie tins! You might tie the proverbial string around your finger each time you take a pie home for the family.*

When the Doors Closed at Night

Okay, so you can remember all of the great things about shopping at Wolf and Dessauer, like picking out just the right gift or the perfect new dress, and watch the co-workers wrap it up just right. I'm sure you can close your eyes and remember all of the sights and sounds that were going on around you as you left with your purchase, already looking forward to your next shopping trip. But did you ever wonder what went on at night after the lights went out and the doors were locked? After the escalator made its last run? After the tearoom and the cafeteria served their last hungry customers and the security guard turned the key in the lock?

From looking through old store material and newsletters, it became pretty clear that Wolf and Dessauer never rested. In fact, a whole other group of co-workers began their shift, and maybe theirs were the most important jobs of all. They were the people who worked hard behind the scenes to keep Wolf and Dessauer the great place it was.

First, there were the security guards who cleared the cash registers to get them ready for the next day. Then there was the housekeeping crew that started cleaning in the basement and moved upward, floor by floor, cleaning, vacuuming, shining and polishing. Of course, they would pay special attention to the kitchens, which were always spotless.

Shortly after midnight, the bakers would come to the tearoom kitchens. They would work all night to prepare the cakes, rolls, donuts and breads that would be used in the Gourmet Bake Shop and the restaurants in the store. Except for two of the bakers, James Deeds and Athanasios Dimovitis, all of the other cooks were women. Early in the wee hours of the morning, the "pie ladies" would arrive. These ladies were responsible for baking about six

Where Fort Wayne Shopped

The W&D tearoom welcoming visiting teachers in town for a convention. *Authors' collection.*

A box containing one of W&D's famous Easter bonnets. *Courtesy of Sue Hackleman.*

hundred pies every week. About that same time, the meat cooks would start their work. About two hundred gallons of soup was made every week, and up to two thousand pounds of meat and poultry was prepared and served to the Wolf and Dessauer patrons.

Complimentary packets of matches for the customers of W&D. *Courtesy of Sue Hackleman.*

But the work didn't stop there. At dawn, trucks would arrive at the dock with fresh produce and other supplies, such as eight hundred heads of lettuce and twenty gallons of cream, just for one week of cooking.

Wolf and Dessauer also employed a vegetable cook, salad cooks, a coffee and dessert girl and a sandwich girl. All of these ladies started their day in the early morning hours. Not leaving anything out, an entire dish crew would arrive at 7:00 a.m. to clean up after the night cooking and baking.

Pantry girls would then start brewing the morning coffee, more than ten thousand cups per week for consumption throughout the store. As it approached 8:00 a.m., the security guards and morning housekeeping crews would start beautifying Wolf and Dessauer's outer façade by sweeping the sidewalks, putting up the flag and cleaning and shining the entrances so that the store was bright and elegant for the day's business and its customers.

Nothing was ever forgotten or done in anything less than a perfect way. It was like an elegant lady getting ready for an important party, and this is the reason your memories of this wonderful store are so exact. The details were important, and the staff paid attention to every one of them.

THE GOLDEN RULES

COMMUNITY SERVICE

With the management of Wolf and Dessauer aspiring to bring the very best of capabilities to their work, they also inspired their employees to do the same. It would also naturally follow that the employees of Wolf and Dessauer would then follow the example of Mr. G. Irving Latz and be involved in their community. One of the ways they did this was to participate in blood drives. In fact, they were so dedicated to these drives that some of them donated more than one gallon of blood, for which they received a special recognition pin.

In the mid-1960s, Nelson K. Neiman was the chairman of the board of Wolf and Dessauer. He was another to set a fine example of selfless giving. In 1966, he received his gallon donation pin along with co-worker Oleta Crouse. What is even more amazing is that during that same spring, three co-workers received their *two-gallon* pins: Arinetta Manning, manager of the book department; Paul Cooper, manager of housewares; and Edgar Thomas, driver. Even though we are talking about events that happened nearly forty years ago, we think that these co-workers deserve to be mentioned and thanked once again.

Knowing what we've learned about Wolf and Dessauer, we shouldn't be surprised to hear that it was one of the first companies to adopt a family for Christmas, much like the program the Christmas Bureau puts on today.

The Christmas fund came from all of the departments in the store. The co-workers donated their own funds and also raised money in various ways. We know—but are uncertain of some of the details—that sometime during the 1940s, Mr. Alan Bixby, who was the display director, ran the program and actually made a display in the store of the wonderful items that were going to be purchased for the adopted family.

CUSTOMER SERVICE

There is a little psychology in every career that involves selling or in any kind of marketing. Every individual is different, but when shopping, people can be classified into groups. Wolf and Dessauer co-workers were taught about the following types of customers and then given the suggestions in order to make their shopping experience more pleasurable and meaningful. Here are a few of those tips:

- The uncertain, hesitating customer who finds it difficult to decide just what she wants. *Ask her questions that will help you determine her needs and then suggest merchandise that will fill these needs. Be sure of your own knowledge of merchandise and give her that assistance she needs.*
- The customer who is in hurry. *She is usually quite sure just what she wants and can be pleased most by giving her quick, helpful service.*
- The customer with an inferiority complex. *She says nothing and is terribly worried that she might make a mistake. Ask her questions to get her opinion. It will make her feel important and that her suggestions are well worth making.*
- The last type is easiest because they already know-it-all. *Let her do most of the talking. Ask her opinion; let her tell you what is best, and she will probably talk herself into buying. With a little practice, you can judge a person accurately and quickly, and your sales volume will mount with each customer.*

This lesson in the psychology of sales came from the Wolf and Dessauer personnel training department and was given in 1950. Whereas most department store employees undergo an initial training process, Wolf and Dessauer co-workers attended training classes throughout the year. They were constantly learning and refining their customer skills. This is an excerpt from an actual lesson plan for a 1952 training class, written by Mary Schaub:

ATTENTIVENESS:

To be attentive, you must look attentive. A co-worker who is slouching on the counter, discussing last night's date or half-heartedly doing some stock work, will never make a hit with a customer. Remember that we are all here for one purpose, to serve the customer. She is our real boss, and she must have our undivided attention while we are serving her.

When a customer enters our department, recognize her with a friendly greeting and then give her your full attention, making her problem your major interest at the moment.

Some customers shop here because of the name on the box, some for the label inside of a dress, and some because they know they can return the merchandise if it isn't right and we will make it right.

All of our customers expect more in our store. The added services we give our customer's and the careful attention given to them by our co-workers makes the difference. Let's see that they get this attention in full measure.

The following article is from the July 1945 *Co-Worker*:

KEEP SMILING

When a customer is waiting and you cannot speed the sale you're making turn to the waiting customer, nod and SMILE.

When you're busy and a customer is waiting for you, nod our recognition that she is there and SMILE.

When nothing will please a fussy customer, be patient, apologize if necessary and use care when you smile, but SMILE.

Don't expect a smile in return. You may get it. If not, don't sulk. Your smiles, properly adjusted to suit the time and problem, will make your customer easier to satisfy. And, you'll find you'll be easier to satisfy and you'll be smiling more often after each customer has left. If done right, your after-sale smile can become a broad grin.

Reading this just reminds how lacking this kind of customer service is today. With everyone rushing around trying to complete the next item on their to-do list, no one wants to wait on line or be made to feel invisible. A nod of recognition and a smile would be a small but effective antidote. Wolf and Dessauer salespeople had the right idea:

I am a little thing with a big meaning. I help everybody. I unlock doors, open hearts, do away with prejudices. I create friendship and goodwill. I inspire respect. I bore nobody. I violate no law. I cost nothing. Many have praised me, none have condemned me. I am pleasing to everyone. I am useful every moment of the day. I am Courtesy.

Are you a model co-worker? The following article came from a 1947 written survey taken at Wolf and Dessauer. Co-workers were to designate ten qualities most desirable in fellow co-workers. How would you rate yourself?

- Is congenial and happy on the job.
- Observes store rules and regulations.
- Willingly works as a member of the team and doesn't have to be a "star."
- Shows respect for the stock of other co-workers.
- Willingly does his/her share of stock work.
- Is considerate of the feelings of other co-workers.
- Never grabs sales.
- Is willing to help others in emergencies.
- Will treat my customers in my absence as I would treat them.
- Is willing to do more than just "get by."

Wolf and Dessauer took care to keep its co-workers highly educated, not only in what was new and trendy in their own departments but also, more importantly, in how to be a better salesperson and assistant to the customer. As mentioned earlier, training classes went on through the year, but articles appeared monthly in the employee newsletter, and we found them fascinating. It wouldn't hurt if they were reprinted for employee manuals of today:

TAKE PRIDE IN SELLING

The role of the salesperson has always been a starring one in world affairs. Back through the ages, generals have had to sell their men on the concept of victory at a price; rulers and statesmen have sold entire countries their ideologies and we mustn't forget the most persuasive salesmen of all, the explorers and inventors, purveyors of the new and different.

Today's salespeople may never have the opportunity to sell a fabulous new world to a queen, but their opportunities in this era of the "bigger mousetrap" are unlimited! As a direct contributor to industrial progress, the importance of selling as a vocation is unquestioned. It has been said that a sales force is probably the most important investment in a company's portfolio. And we might add that an army of well-trained, intelligent salespeople is a vital factor in a nation's march to prosperity and to a higher standard of living.

Another function of the salesperson, which is often not considered, is his contribution to public welfare and a better way of living. Conscientious and sincere salesmanship may frequently influence, to a great extent, the customer's tastes and thus may actually raise his standards of living. This lifting of standards and forming of new desires also creates an individual, for after all, isn't it the desire for newer and finer things, for a more gracious way of life, which incites an individual to obtain and hold better and still better jobs?

From the economic and social standpoint, selling is an essential vocation and when handled with due respect and dignity, one of which to be very proud.

SATISFIED CUSTOMERS

Dear Sirs:

Last Tuesday I took a few of my friends to Fort Wayne to shop, and spent most of the day in your store. It was lovely, neat and clean and I don't know when I have had such courteous clerks wait on me.

I knew you would be happy to know what was going on behind the scenes and you can rest assured we certainly got the attention we used to get in all stores.

Rest assured, we will be back soon again!

–anonymous customer, 1965

Dear Sirs:

I am writing to you concerning a Wilton Velvet rug my parents bought from you in 1915. No, this is not a complaint, just a story of a rug and a little more. This rug graced our "parlor" for the first years and then the living room as long as my parents lived. Then it passed into my brother's possession, and is still in use in the living room of his summer home. How does it look now in 1967? Great! The color in the beautiful design is clear and bright and no visible wear is apparent after all these years of use.

The rug has proved the advantage of good versus poor quality. Through the years, Wolf and Dessauer have proved their dependability. As a result our family has bought not a little and have appreciated your gracious salespeople of whom I can mention Mr. Koeneman and Mr. Miller, in your Appliance Department.

Thank you for letting me express myself,

-anonymous customer, 1967

THE CUSTOMER SERVICE DEPARTMENT

Until the late 1930s, all adjustments, returns or exchanges were made "over the counter." In 1939, Bob Zahrt was made manager of a new adjustment desk that was later expanded into the customer relations department. Mr. Zahrt knew from the example that management set, since the first day the store opened, that a happy customer will always result in return sales.

Wolf and Dessauer co-workers were trained to believe that all people coming into the store arrived with some kind of problem. Perhaps it was a service problem, a budget problem or just not knowing what to buy. They were taught that the co-worker's main function was to discover the problem and do whatever was necessary to resolve it as courteously and promptly as possible.

Management encouraged employees to put themselves in the customer's shoes, thinking how they would want the problem to be solved. Whether the transaction was for something as simple and inexpensive as a greeting card or as extravagant as a mink coat, customers were made to feel as though their contact with each co-worker had been a pleasant, friendly experience.

While walking down the street one day, Mr. Zahrt was stopped by a police officer, who said, "You probably don't remember me, but eight years ago you took care of our complaint about a suite of furniture. You were so good about handling the problems to our satisfaction our family hasn't shopped at any other store since."

That was a fine example of the confidence Fort Wayne shoppers had in Wolf and Dessauer. Safeguarding that confidence was the main function of the customer relations department.

REMEMBERING CO-WORKERS

Talking to people about Wolf and Dessauer is always one of our favorite things to do, but talking to people who worked at the store is especially heartwarming for us. The people who were employed by Wolf and Dessauer share an elite group of memories that is different than any others because they saw the store from the inside. They were there in the quiet hours before the opening of the great doors and after they closed. They knew an entirely different world that only they can share with us, so we wanted to share the memories of some of the co-workers with you. Some are from the Wolf and Dessauer employee newsletters, some information is gathered from friends and families and some are from personal interviews. No matter how the information was obtained, we hope you'll enjoy and maybe even recognize someone you know.

Employee Spotlight:
Looking Back Through the Years

1947

Adelaide Hammer was welcomed to the buying staff of Wolf and Dessauer in 1947. She was appointed buyer for sportswear on the third floor and came to W&D from Donaldson's of Minneapolis.

What made Miss Hammer a great pick for the folks at W&D was her many years of merchandising experience, which she gained at Lord & Taylors in New York City. She had held many positions there, including manager and buyer of the Women's Uniform Shop.

Miss Hammer was the seventh female officer to be commissioned in the Marine Corps in World War II. She held the rank of captain for three and a half years. During that time, she was in charge of the clothing for the entire Marine Corps of eighteen thousand women! Most of her military career was spent in the United States; however, she did make several inspection tours to Pearl Harbor.

Dorothy Reed began her employment behind the counter at the Wolf and Dessauer fountain. Shortly after that, she was promoted to cashier.

At the time of her interview for the June 1947 issue of the *Co-Worker*, Dorothy said her favorite pastimes outside of work were her passion for gardening, both indoors and out, and her love of vacationing in northern Michigan.

When asked if being around all of the delectable "yummies" that were always so abundant in the fountain was a problem for her, she quickly provided that "food was the least of my worries" and then hastened to add that the ten pounds she gained in the first three months of her employment at W&D were a testimony to the wonderful food!

The names of two more co-workers, Laura Snowberger and Fred Daesler, were added to the Wolf and Dessauer retirement list in February 1947.

Anyone who ever browsed around the main floor during the 1940s will remember statuesque, white-haired Laura Snowberger. She was a faithful co-worker in the leather goods department ever since her employment began in 1932.

Fred Daesler was on the job at Wolf and Dessauer for forty years. Mr. Daesler first came to Wolf and Dessauer in 1907 and was connected with the shipping department for his entire employment.

Records like these two fine co-workers just go to prove that there was nowhere else like W&D.

1965

Seven new members were inducted into Wolf and Dessauer's "25 Year Club." They were honored at the annual day of recognition in June at a tearoom luncheon. The store gave each of them a watch and a gold twenty-five-year pin. Those who were honored this day were Elroy Miller, Division C manager; James Smith, furniture department; Dale Ferguson, Division E manager; Edward Trentman, department manager (basement); Ogereta Steck, domestics basement store; Virginia Gale, department manager; and Marguerite McGuire, millinery department.

Year Uncertain

Dreams do come true! Years ago, when Louise Dellinger lived out of town and her children were small, she always shopped at Wolf and Dessauer. Her dream was to work here one day. She remembers being impressed with the store's "elegant" look and the high caliber of its salespeople, thinking that "no other stores can match the W&D atmosphere."

Louise's statement: "I don't call it a job, W&D is a wonderful place to spend forty hours a week because I don't think of the people I help as customers but rather as friends and every day I try real hard to make three or four new ones." That sums up the philosophy that makes the charming and successful Louise Dellinger a source of pleasure for her customers in the sportswear department.

Louise has been with W&D for twelve years. She believes the most important thing in her selling is to first sell yourself, and then you can sell our merchandise—concentrate not on the dollar but on the customer. Even when she wraps her merchandise, she takes extra care that the opening of the package should be a delight to the customer and carry the W&D touch.

Everyone has a motive for working. Hers is for the education of her children. Her son has been on the dean's list for the last eight years and has now graduated with a doctorate in dentistry. Her daughter will be in college this year and then on to nurses training for three years.

Louise says that the store executives have been so good to her, as though they are her "home away from home" family. If she ever needed any personal help, she feels she could call on them. She appreciates the friendliness and cooperation of the co-workers with whom she is in daily contact. As Louise says, "My day is never boring! As it ends, I feel maybe I have pleased a new customer or renewed a friendship with an old friend."

KEN LUCAS: THE WOLF AND DESSAUER YEARS, 1960–1964

Searching everywhere for photos to use for this book, we were happily surprised to find Ken Lucas and his cache of wonderful pictures. Much to our amazement, Ken had also written down his remembrances from his time as a W&D co-worker and gave us permission to retell them in this book.

During the spring and early summer of 1960, I was employed at Stillman's Department Store in the shoe department. Working in retail sales was enjoyable because you met so many nice people, and when they bought something, everyone was happy. However, the desire to work for the best store in town got the better of me, and I decided that I wanted to work for the largest, most distinguished department store in Fort Wayne: Wolf and Dessauer.

At the interview, I was asked what I would like to do. I responded, "I would like to work in the men's clothing department because I like to sell to men." It was a surprise to hear that the majority of shoppers in men's clothing were actually women!

An unbelievable opportunity was then presented. They were interested in developing a new Camera Department and needed someone to make it happen. That was the easiest decision of my life. They had started selling some film and boxed Brownie cameras on one display case, located in the Sporting Goods Department on the main floor. It was near the bottom of the escalator coming down from the second floor. Annual sales were around $3,000.

There were two plans: send me to the Eastman Kodak Sales Training School in Rochester, New York, and build a completely new department by the Men's Shoe Department on the back wall in the northeast corner of the store. This location would force customers to walk through the entire store to simply drop off and pick up film.

In August, they sent me to Rochester for two weeks on a train, leaving from the Superior Street Station. Back then, the rails made the *clickitty-clack* sound that either put you to sleep or kept you awake, depending on your mood. I shared a room in an older downtown hotel with a nice guy named Lyle from down south. We had a good time. Other than the Kodak Company, the only thing I remember about Rochester was the large neon "Genesee Beer" signs and the beautiful hotel.

The Kodak Company was enormous! They were a city within a city and could operate entirely with nothing from the city of Rochester. Everyone was not only very professional but also a lot of fun. They knew how to make learning enjoyable.

The first weekend, they gave us their best cameras with all the accessories and all of the film we wanted and put us on a bus to Niagara Falls. We spent the day shooting hundreds of pictures, which were all developed for free! Back in class, we then discussed everything possible about the pictures we had taken. Those two weeks were an unforgettable experience.

By Christmas, we were operational in the new department. What an experience! The first year we hit $9,000 in sales, the second year $25,000. In the third year we reached $60,000 in sales and in the fourth year close to $100,000. With two part-time employees, we won the annual contest for the largest increase in sales for our division each year.

By 1962, we had grown into the largest Polaroid dealer in Allen County. The free Polaroid classes were a great success. Customers would come to the store conference room, where we would have coffee and cookies, give them a free roll of film and let them take pictures of the lovely models that we hired. We would then review their pictures, give them pointers and answer any questions they might have.

The buyer that had the Camera Department also had the Sporting Goods and Luggage Department, so I frequently got the opportunity to sell in those departments. A delightful lady named Mary Olsen ran the luggage department. The Sporting Goods Department was located at the bottom of the escalators in a very busy area. Everyone coming down from the second floor looked directly at the sporting goods displays while they were riding down the escalator.

Two new items on the market then were "Pitch Back" and "Tackraw." One was a tightly stretched net that would bounce a pitched ball back to you, and the other was a wicker "scoop" on a handle. The buyer decided to make us take turns throwing a ball into the net using the Tackraw and catching it when it bounced back. That was one of the hardest things I ever had to do. Trying to look cool in the busiest part of the store, in front of the wealthiest people in town, was embarrassing. Occasionally, I would miss the ball, and it would roll down the escalator to the basement. Everyone enjoyed that but me. However, sales were unbelievable. One of us would take our turn on the Tackraw while another clerk would ring up the sales.

Another interesting thing about the escalators was the kids' untied shoestrings would get caught in the steps, and the parents would panic when they got to the bottom. We had a pair of pliers at the corner of the department and would use them to yank the shoestrings free whenever it happened.

We were required to attend training classes before starting to work there. I remember three parts of the classes: how to sell, the customer was always right and techniques of the shoplifter. If you got upset with a customer, you would be fired. The one exception was if they started cursing; you were allowed to excuse yourself and get your supervisor.

My department was next to the Men's Shoe Department. Harry Kennard and Louie Koch ran that department. Harry kept a record of every pair of shoes sold with the customer's name and information on an index card. He must have had a thousand cards. I remember when business was slow; they would sit in their office and call people on the phone to see if they could drum up business. I know that the top men in Fort Wayne bought their shoes from Harry and Louie, and they knew them all.

Next to the shoe department was a shoe shine stand. A younger, one-legged black man shined shoes at the two-chair stand. He did not have an artificial leg, so he used a crutch. He would stand on one leg with the crutch under the other arm for hours shining shoes. There were a lot of days that he probably made more money than I did.

It's funny how you always remember the eating places. During the summer, they opened a French Café outside on the sidewalk on the Wayne Street side, closer to Barr Street. What a delightful place to eat.

I believe there was a very nice restaurant on the second floor with white table cloths, but I don't remember eating there. There was also a snack bar in the basement near the up-escalators, with stools around the counter. Behind the snack bar was the employees' cafeteria, down the hallway between the snack bar and the Photography Studio. In that hallway, they would put a picture and some information about the employee of the week. If you were picked, it included a picture from the studio and lunch with one of the executives. That was a big week for me, once.

They set up a few televisions in the store during John Glenn's first orbital flight on February 20, 1962. During the recovery, everyone—customers and employees—gathered around to watch it on the TV. There were sixty to seventy people watching near our department alone. The store came to a standstill.

There were two "floorwalkers" that I knew. The shorter one always looked the same so shoplifters would see her and know she was on duty. The taller one looked different every day so they would not recognize her. I don't think I ever saw her wear the same clothes twice, and her style changed all the time.

On the afternoon of February 13, 1962, I was told to get some cameras and go down the street to the old Wolf and Dessauer building because it was on fire. The building at the corner of Clinton and Washington was already engulfed. The first report was called in as "W&D is on fire," so the fire department went to the new store first. As far as I can recall, no one ever asked to see the films. I still have some of them.

One day, I walked over to the cashier in the Men's Clothing Department to get change. There was a nice floor model record player, with a set of headphones lying on top. I picked them up, and when I put them on, it was the most unbelievable sound that I ever heard. One of the salespeople told me it was called "stereo." How things have changed since then.

Store hours were 9:00 a.m. to 5:00 p.m., Monday through Saturday. We stayed open until 9:00 p.m. on Wednesday evenings and were always closed on Sunday. Days off were Sunday and your choice of Tuesday or Thursday. I always took off Thursdays.

We lived at 628 Anderson Street off Spy Run. It was over a mile to the store, but I walked it when I could, not to save gas but to save the parking cost downtown. I think gas was less than forty cents a gallon. One day it was rainy so I drove, but it was nice when I left work so I walked home. When I came down the street, I thought that someone had stolen my car since it was missing until I remembered that I drove that day. I learned not to do that again.

My pay at Stillman's was $1.00 per hour. Starting pay at W&D's was $1.25 per hour, but within six months I was making $1.50 per hour. I earned $60.00 per week. After taxes, savings club and a washer payment, my take-home pay amounted to about $40.00 per week.

It was the allure of big bucks that finally pulled me away from Wolf and Dessauer. In 1964, I joined Zollner Pistons at a rate of $2.85 per hour and within ninety days was earning over $3.00 per hour. Keep in mind that was triple my income from Stillman's only four years earlier. Those were the good times.

The Wolf and Dessauer employees were some of the friendliest, most professional and nicest people that I've ever met. The customers were generally the most respectable in town and always a pleasure to meet. I never remember a confrontation or unpleasant event during the entire time that I was part of the Wolf and Dessauer family.

With much appreciation, we thank Mr. Lucas for his story, but even more than that we thank him for all of the beautiful photographs and slides he allowed us to use from his personal collection. The majority of the beautiful photos throughout this book are thanks to his generosity. And thank you, too, to his son, Eric, for helping us get in touch with his dad.

The W&D Orchestra

So, we know that Wolf and Dessauer was head and shoulders above any other retailer of its day. We know about the many wonderful things it did for the community and its co-workers both in and out of the workplace, and we know that the people at W&D liked to have fun. But did you know that W&D had its own orchestra?

In 1948, some rumors around the store had begun about a lot of musical talent floating around. Some co-workers had actually heard about the orchestra but had never actually heard it play. One Tuesday afternoon after work, a group of co-workers got together and slipped into the auditorium to listen to a practice session.

Musicians included Eugene Myers (who was a teenage son of LaMora Myers) on the bass fiddle, Mr. Cameron on drums, Alan Bixby of display department fame on the violin (he was also sometimes seen strolling around the toy department playing), Emerson Miller on the saxophone and William Brosler on the tenor banjo. Also involved were pianists Cleo Kramer and Lucille Mumaugh. The W&D orchestra made its debut that same year and played at many W&D functions.

FOND MEMORIES

This book would never be complete without including memories from the people who loved Wolf and Dessauer the most, the people who lived in Fort Wayne and the people who came from miles away to shop there. We'd like you to relax a while and see if this chapter brings some good memories back to you.

As for me, my fondest memory involves a yo-yo. When I was a kid in kindergarten, I sent away some Campbell's soup labels to get a wooden top and yo-yo set in the mail. The day after I received them, I took my yo-yo to class to show it off.

My class was divided up into eight tables of about four kids each, all sitting together, and when I put the yo-yo down on the table, the kid sitting next to me grabbed it and started sliding it back and forth to the other kids in the class. When my teacher saw the distraction, she confiscated the yo-yo, and I never saw it again. I was so proud of my new toy and now it was gone.

Later that Christmas season, my mom took me to Wolf and Dessauer to talk to Santa, and I remember asking him for a number of things, but most of all I remember asking him to see if he could get me a replacement for my Campbell's yo-yo.

Lo and behold, on Christmas morning, when I looked under the tree, there was a small package and it was my precious yo-yo! When I asked Santa for "some surprises," little did I know I would be so surprised on Christmas morning! He really was the "real Santa."

–Maurice Doyle House, Pleasant Lake, Indiana

I only worked at Wolf and Dessauer for two or three years, from 1953 through 1956, but really thought it was a great place. I worked in the Bridal Salon. Norma Roembke was the buyer. She did a lot of pretty weddings and had some funny incidents. Evelyn Abbott was the bridal coordinator. They are probably deceased now.

–Luanne Oberyfell, Fort Wayne, Indiana

I started with Wolf and Dessauer as a management trainee in the summer of 1957 following my graduation from Earlham College in Richmond, Indiana. I was an assistant buyer in Boys' Wear to Dick Meyers and then in Men's Furnishings to Harry Bleeke. Both of them were tremendous merchants from whom I learned the fundamentals of department store retailing. After eight months I was hired by Uncle Sam to spend a few years in uniform, and I returned to Wolf and Dessauer in February 1960 to the new store location, where I spent the next six years as buyer of ladies coats, suits, furs and "smart money" dresses. In the summer of 1966, I moved my family to Wisconsin when I became affiliated with the H.C. Prange Co., a four-store chain of department stores, which eventually grew to twenty-four stores.

I will never forget the wonderful associations I had with the co-workers at Wolf and Dessauer. I am honored to have been a part of one of the classiest organizations in the entire department store industry. Bud and Bill Latz, Nelson Nieman and the corps of managers they led were top-flight people. Few, if any, stores in America could equal the caliber of service offered by the really professional sales associates in the Wolf and Dessauer store. The integrity of sale events was unlike anything I have seen since.

I often hear people lament the passing of those good old days, when the finest stores gave real services. I can always look back with pride that I was, even though for only a few years, a part of one of the best: the Wolf and Dessauer store. Congratulations to you who are responsible for capturing the memories of this great store.

–Tom Hamilton, Green Bay, Wisconsin

Well, first of all, I remember Wolf and Dessauer. It was the big store at Christmastime. Santa Claus would be there, Phil Steigerwald. I would pass there every day going down to Calhoun and Berry to do my "Man on the Street" program called *One Moment Please*. Then I would come back and go through W&D.

I had many interview programs in W&D on the third floor, but some in the basement. I would be talking to Santa and interviewing the children. To see these children and the way their eyes would light up while they sat on Santa's lap was wonderful. That was the big thing at Christmastime, to visit Santa at Wolf and Dessauer.

Of course, I also remember Wolf and Dessauer from many shopping experiences, but the main thing was Christmastime and all the windows decorated with moving toys.

–Bob Sievers, radio personality, WOWO

I remember being about four years old and waiting in line at Wolf and Dessauer to see Santa Claus. I would go down every year and talk to Santa and wait in line just enchanted with all the wonderful decorations, plus the TV cameras.

Every weekday at 4:30 p.m., the TV station would do a half-hour show about children talking with Santa. When I wasn't in line, I was at home watching to see if I knew any of the kids. One year, they put the camera right on my face for a long time, and so many people mentioned to my mother that they had seen her beautiful daughter on TV.

–Barb Richards, program director, WAJI

I remember being a child and just being mesmerized by that place. I remember the store had a plastic tube system that the staff would use to send things back and forth to the office. It was so much fun watching the stuff go through the tube. It went so fast! I also remember those Christmas windows and how crowded it was out front of the store. It was really cold, but I didn't want to budge until I had absorbed everything!

–Linda McCoy, Fort Wayne, Indiana

I remember playing on the escalators and the clerks yelling at me all the time. I also remember buying Christmas gifts for the family and standing in awe of the windows. My brother appeared on his fifth or sixth birthday with Santa Claus. We always watched the show at Christmastime.

–Sharyn A. Harmeer, Fort Wayne, Indiana

Although we shopped at other stores, it seemed like most of our department store purchases were made at Wolf and Dessauer. It truly was a special place. It was quite elegant. And the elevators run by gloved operators who announced the floors, and what was on each floor fascinated me. I wish I could remember what was on each floor. I liked going to the mezzanine and looking out over the store. The escalators were fun to ride, too. The store always seemed to be busy with lots of shoppers, and we always had to dress nicely to go downtown. It seemed so special.

There was a tube system that was used to send information to the business department and did indeed seem to work fast. On rare occasions, my grandmother and I had lunch in the Tea Room. That was a real treat. Later, when I was in high school at North Side, my friends and I would ride the bus from my grandmother's house downtown. We'd shop and, once in a while, include the Tea Room as part of our trip. However, our budget didn't permit this often. Perhaps hamburgers and fries were more to our liking.

Since my mother and grandmother sewed all of our clothes, we frequently went to the yard goods floor. When I was little, this was very boring and dull. I was more fascinated by the little girls' pretty dresses. But of course, they were out of my parents' budget. By the time my mother finished our clothes, they were truly special and one of a kind.

When I was in late elementary school, I joined a 4-H club. Our family had moved onto St. Joe Center Road by then. Not surprisingly, I took up sewing as one of my many projects. I frequently purchased the material at W&D. I turned out to be a pretty good seamstress and won many Allen County Fair awards. W&D donated some of the prizes, and I have several silver pieces from the store and an original tan W&D box.

The toy store was a most delightful place. At Christmas, there was a huge operating train display that one could view. When I was twelve, I finally saved enough money to buy a fourteen-inch "grown-up" doll from the store. I still have the doll, although she has a new wig. I no longer have the original clothes. But the real treasure was the decorated holiday windows. I can say that while looking at those displays you were truly transported to a fantasyland. I especially liked the Santa workshop scenes.

I have visited other large department stores in other cities like Detroit, Chicago and Philadelphia but was never really impressed. I think it was because we had such a large elegant store right here in our own town. I shop at the mall now, and it just isn't the same.

–Janet Ormiston, Fort Wayne, Indiana

In 1960, I came to Fort Wayne from Lima, Ohio, and I was a freshman in college and had never been to a big department store. After my folks moved me into the dormitory, the first place we went was downtown so I could see downtown Fort Wayne. My eyes just bugged out of my head when I walked in W&D because in Lima we had just two stores, but nothing nearly as big!

Where Fort Wayne Shopped

I remember that my mom, who was feeling really bad because I was the first child to leave home, promised she would buy me something in that store. My parents were not wealthy. But I remember seeing a sweater for nineteen dollars, and that was a huge price in 1960. It was for my family anyway. It was beautiful. It was all beautifully knit and we bought it. I wore it for years. In college, everybody wanted to borrow it. I wore it for several years, and believe it or not, my daughter wore it years later. It was the favorite sweater of my whole life. Not just because it was a beautiful sweater but because of the memories connected with my first time at Wolf and Dessauer.

Another thing, I worked at a different store for spending money. My parents paid for my college, but I made money to spend, and after we would have a huge exam, our gift to ourselves was to take a bus downtown from Rudisill Blvd. to W&D, and that was our treat for having done well on a test or a semester. Wolf and Dessauer has huge memories for me. Just a lot of fun times.

–Char Binkley, WBCL Radio

One of my favorite memories was of the Wee WanD shop. I had bought my mother a beautiful green scarf. Well, it was beautiful to a nine-year-old anyway. They boxed it up and wrapped it up for me really prettily. I couldn't wait until Christmas to give that scarf to my mother, so I practically forced it on her when we got home, begging her to open the package.

After spending a long time trying to get me to change my mind and wait until Christmas, she finally gave in an opened it and "ooohhed" and "ahhed" appropriately over the wonderful gift. Realizing then that I had just given my mother the only Christmas gift I had for her, I started to cry, wondering why I had done that! I think I really ruined it for her.

–Donna McEvoy, Fort Wayne, Indiana

I remember the models that were all dressed up. I was about twelve. I thought they were gorgeous. They wore all the newest fashions and just walked around the store so elegantly. They all looked like movie stars. I thought that must be the neatest job in the world.

–Sue Schuman, Fort Wayne, Indiana

Everyone I knew shopped at Wolf and Dessauer. It was a big deal to go downtown and shop there. I can remember my mother buying stockings. The salesgirl would bring out these flat little boxes and would open them up and gently put her hand inside the stocking to show the color and how sheer they were. My mother would buy one pair every week. I think it was just an excuse to have to go to W&D again to buy more.

–S. Arnold, Fort Wayne, Indiana

When I was about ten, my mother took me to Wolf and Dessauer to buy a winter coat. I was a chubby kid, and the regular kid sizes didn't fit me, so my mother had to take me to the ladies department. I was pretty embarrassed that I needed to have a ladies size-sixteen coat, but the salesgirl was so nice to me I remember her to this day.

After that, my mother took me to the cafeteria and bought me a big sundae. Is it any wonder I couldn't fit into kid's size clothing?

–Deb Crandall, Fort Wayne, Indiana

I remember my mom taking me to lunch at the Tea Room for my birthday. Wow! Talk about classy!

–B. Bushings, Evansville, Indiana

Walking by the window displays at Christmastime was pretty thrilling. My favorite was the little girl with the long blond braids who was baking cookies in a tiny oven. Every time she opened the door, a puff of "smoke" would come out.

–E. Hastings, Decatur, Indiana

We lived in Anderson when I was little, but I had an aunt in Fort Wayne. Every year, mom and dad would pile us into our old Chevy and make the trip to Fort Wayne. It seemed like it took hours, but the night we got there, they would take us and my cousins downtown to Wolf and Dessauer. I would stand at those windows like a zombie with my nose smashed up against the glass. My parents had to push me to move along to the next window because I stood there so long I held everyone up. After that night, it really was Christmastime for us.

–Kyle Reed, Marion, Indiana

I felt rich going to Wolf and Dessauer. I would pretend I was one of the models walking around the store and hold my hand out in graceful gestures like I saw them doing. I don't think I ever fooled anyone, though. I was only seven!

–K. Hunnicutt, Fort Wayne, Indiana

Where Fort Wayne Shopped

I bought my prom dress at Wolf and Dessauer. It was baby-blue chiffon with a wraparound stole. It's still in my closet, and I think of Wolf and Dessauer every time I see it. I wish my daughter and granddaughters would have had a place to shop like I did. I will never forget it. I still remember the beautiful smells at the perfume counter.

−V. Meron, Huntington, Indiana

I remember the banana splits at the cafeteria. They were great! I also remember falling down the escalator once. It didn't hurt as much as it embarrassed me when I noticed one of the store models nearby.

−T. Schmidt, New Haven, Indiana

I have a funny memory. Well, it's funny now, but back then my mother wanted to die of embarrassment. I had just gotten done eating a hotdog down the street one Saturday, and my mom had taken my brother and me to see Santa at W&D. I was so nervous, I got sick all over Santa. I heard my mother gasp. I am so thankful that moment was not on TV!

−J. Guttenburg, Fort Wayne, Indiana

When I was a kid, I used to love to go downtown with my family on a Saturday. That always included a trip to Wolf and Dessauer. I remember thinking it was really odd that they kept their leather stuff, like gloves and wallets and things, in the jewelry department in glass cases. Looking back, I guess that was pretty smart. It was probably to prevent shoplifting.

−E. Hamilton, Fort Wayne, Indiana

When my grandmother died, my sister and I had to go through all of her stuff. It was kind of a sad day for us. Then we found an old hatbox from Wolf and Dessauer. Inside of it were two of her "Sunday" hats and a bunch of old love letters. We sat there reading the letters, looking at the hats. It brought back so many great childhood memories, it really cheered us up. My sister and I still have one of those hats each.

−K. Martin, Fort Wayne, Indiana

My mom used to work at Wolf and Dessauer, and after school sometimes we would go visit her. After we said hello to her, we would head straight for the cafeteria and those big cookies they used to make. I remember it so vividly. Poor mom, she always thought we were coming just to see her!

−D. Crown, Fort Wayne, Indiana

I bought my daughter's first baby outfit there. I loved that store!

—Pam Bangert, Fort Wayne, Indiana

In the summer of 1943, I was working at Baer Field. I had gotten off work, and being a young woman in my twenties, I went shopping in downtown Fort Wayne to Wolf and Dessauer. My last name at the time was "Wolff," but we were from Germany and not related to the "Wolf" in Wolf and Dessauer. The Latz family owned the store. Bill Latz was a high school friend. We went to Central High. I graduated in 1939, and I believe Bill graduated in 1940.

At the time, we also had the Grand Leader, Earl Groth, Paris, Fishman's and Frank's, but Wolf and Dessauer was tops!

I walked in the front door and headed toward the elevator when a young woman stopped me and said, "We'd like to take your picture." Of course, I said OK. She took me to the mezzanine to the photo department, and they took my picture. People didn't have cameras the way they do now. We didn't have much of anything, so a picture was quite a treat. I felt very important.

I just bought the one picture. I can remember my outfit. It was a white skirt and a white top with red flowers. I must have bought it there at the store. I also remember the lunch counter on the first floor, and their Tea Room upstairs was wonderful. Coming out of the depression years, eating in the Tea Room was pretty high class. The basement always had wonderful buys.

—MaryAmber Bosk, Fort Wayne, Indiana

I remember the Santa Express. My aunt and mom would wait in line to get tickets, and then early on a morning, the train would take us to Columbia City, turn around and come back. Santa would be on the train, come and talk to us as he walked through the cars, and at the end we would get a bag of candy! Everyone was so excited!

I also remember the lighting of the Santa. It was always a delight for me as a child, and when they brought Santa and his reindeer out of storage, we started taking our little children to see it. Their eyes were as big as saucers, and they would scream with glee. Kyle is now twenty-six and Molly is twenty-three, and they still enjoy going to see Santa's bright lights. It wouldn't be Christmas without it.

—Karon Sheehan, Fort Wayne, Indiana

I remember waiting with great anticipation for my turn to peer in those Christmas windows. I believed they were the windows into Santa's world. It seemed like I could stand there for hours, and I really believed they were real. They were so magical. But then my dad would nudge me on down the line until we ran out of windows.

On good years, when Dad's business picked up, we got to go inside to the Wee WanD shop and pick out gifts for our parents. I remember thinking that I was so grown up and special buying my own gifts!

My mom always said that after Wolf and Dessauer closed, she never could replace the "W&D tradition" with anything that was that special. But we had a great time remembering all of this.

–Deana Dennis, Fort Wayne, Indiana

Downtown was the place to go for Christmas. Our parents would take us downtown in the morning, and we would shop all day. That was our time. We would shop at the Wee WanD shop, Murphy's and go to Stillmans and ride the old elevator.

I remember hearing the old Christmas music and seeing the animated characters in the W&D windows and seeing the huge decorated tree on the arch over the street by Murphy's. Those were the days of old and, sadly, only memories now.

My grandmother and uncle would come from Mexico, Indiana, for Thanksgiving on Thanksgiving day. After our big dinner, all eight of us would pile into the station wagon and drive downtown to see the windows, the tree, the wreath and Santa Claus and his reindeer. Of course, all the stores were closed, but what more beauty and entertainment did we need?

–Joetta M. Miller, New Haven, Indiana

When I was about five years old, my dad took me to see Santa at Wolf and Dessauer. Well, I was bashful and wouldn't go up to talk with him. Upon leaving the store, we passed a corner window display with "Santa" shaking his finger at everyone, probably telling everyone to be good, but my dad told me that Santa was disappointed with me for not talking with him. That was about 1948.

There was a little coin shop within Wolf and Dessauer, and my mom would let me pester the coin clerk while she shopped for clothes. Unfortunately, I never could quite afford that 1909S penny for $10.00 that I always wanted.

–Jay Henschen, Fort Wayne, Indiana

My parents took us to Fort Wayne to see the animated Christmas display in Wolf and Dessauer's windows. There was always a big line around the building. It was so much fun!

–Michele Mendenhall, Van Wert, Ohio

I remember my mother having a Wolf and Dessauer charge-a-plate, which predated credit cards. It was steel, similar to a G.I. dog tag, and made by addressograph. The salesperson inserted it into a sort of press, and the customer's name and account number were imprinted on the sales slip. The store kept one copy of the sales slip, and the customer got the other copy. The charge-a-plate was kept in a protective sleeve of leather.

My memories are many, probably monthly trips to Fort Wayne with my mother during my grade school years. We were a family of modest means, but mom always managed to do at least some of her shopping at better stores, primarily at Wolf and Dessauer.

–Robert E. Blank, Van Wert, Ohio

I think Wolf and Dessauer was my favorite store to shop in. That one, and Murphy's, too. Do you remember when they had a "scramble" at Wayne and Calhoun Streets where at a given time everyone could cross the street in any direction? The traffic was stopped in all directions. It was fun.

–Dale R. Schaefer, New Haven, Indiana

I remember the food at the Tearoom. Chicken with yellow gravy and wonderful muffins and chocolate sodas at the fountain. Also, we could get cherry phosphates. I would wear a dress, gloves and a pocketbook and then take the bus downtown for ten cents every Wednesday in the summer time and meet my Aunt Virginia for lunch.

–Linda Brennan Norris, Fort Wayne, Indiana

I grew up in Auburn, and my dad would drive my two older sisters and me down to see the Christmas display. We were really awed by it and disappointed when it stopped.

–Sandra L. Krumma, Fort Wayne, Indiana

I have so many memories. I'm fifty-five, and my mother and I came to Wolf and Dessauer a lot because she loved to shop. She was always dressed up, and we ate in the basement and Tea Room. She was also asked to have her picture taken at W&D. I have it in a bedroom as a keepsake. It makes me realize how much my children (and my grandchildren) are missing today by going to the mall.

–Sue Lantz, Bluffton, Indiana

Where Fort Wayne Shopped

One of the most amazing events was the "Upstairs-Downstairs Sale." This was when items were moved to the basement store and sold at very good clearance prices. Being a novice and having never seen women go crazy over a sale, I was allowed to enter the basement store prior to the sale and watch the women come RUNNING down every stairway there and at full speed, run to a rack of Crystal Room dresses and grab everything in their size.

–Carol Coles, Huntington, Indiana

My father worked at Wolf and Dessauer from 1947 until it closed and then continued on at Ayers. He started out selling men's furnishings in 1947, and from there he became a buyer for the men's furnishing department and would make many buying trips to New York City and Los Angeles to bring back the latest things. Later, Dad became the merchandise manager for the men's departments, and eventually he became the South Town store manager, so my family is really steeped in W&D tradition.

–Beverly Hart, Markle, Indiana

I must have been one of Wolf and Dessauer's youngest and earliest customers. Mr. Latz met us at the door or at the elevator as we arrived. Mother bought wonderful fabrics from a Mr. Green and bought clothes for all of us. Then there were the cane seats on what were probably bentwood chairs in the Tea Room. That was really *the* place to meet. The big brown delivery trucks came long before UPS. I've not lived in Fort Wayne since I went off to college, but I still miss that store, and I still say that many merchants today do not understand that "the Customer is Always Right."

–Phylis Graham Stigall, Scharborough New York

I remember making the annual trek on foot downtown to walk around W&D just to watch the mechanical people in the window. As well I recall my grandmother taking me there just to have a coke from the soda fountain. But the funniest memory I have is watching the women fighting over undergarments when the store went out of business. I couldn't believe how aggressive they were over bloomers.

–Richard Lee Fortier Jr.

I miss W&D; the trip from Hamilton was a long one but worth the time once we got downtown and saw the windows and Santa, not to mention Wee Willie WanD the elf.

–Kim Parker

The winter holidays were very special at Wolf and Dessauer. I always looked forward to the magical merriment that was played out in the windows of the store. Santa's workshop and elves were all made of wood or something that looked like wood, and they were mechanically designed to move like the real things. They were brightly painted and dusted with glitter. I think one year, maybe more, there was a snow queen who turned her head and waved her hand, much to the amusement of those watching. And there were always crowds of people trying to get a peek at the animated scenes. This was big stuff in the '50s, and we loved it.

There was fun to be had all year round at W&D's. After a long day of shopping, my mother and I would go downstairs and take seats at the counter in the coffee shop. My mother would have coffee, and I would get a chocolate soda. For those who have never had the pleasures of this concoction, I'll explain that a chocolate soda is basically chocolate ice cream and soda and maybe a little chocolate syrup. But as a child, I was certain there must have been a special ingredient that made those sodas taste so good.

On rare occasions, we'd go to lunch in the dining room. It was very elegant. They had cloth napkins and silverware that looked like silver (although it wasn't), and they had large velvet ropes strung through short brass pillars. The effect of the ropes was to section off lanes in which you waited to be seated. It's my recollection that if you were a party of one or two you stood in a certain lane. If you needed three or four place settings, you stood in another lane, and really big groups also had a lane of their own.

I don't recall any one thing that I had to eat while in the dining room, but the organization of the place obviously made a big impression on me. The main attraction for me was being allowed to sit with the grownups, and that was exciting. But nothing was better than those chocolate sodas.

–Shelly Long, actress

MEMORIES OF A WAYNEDALE GIRL

Submitted by Carol Richard Brown

I was ten years old when we moved to Fort Wayne from a small town in northern Minnesota. I remember going window shopping with Mom and Aunt Doris. They looked at hats and tried them on. They didn't have much money to spend, so they did mostly looking. Their favorite store was Wolf and Dessauer, and we did our shopping in the basement store. We all wore Ship 'n Shore blouses that retailed at $2.98.

I remember after World War II was over, going to W&D's and standing in line to buy nylons for a gift for my mom. You could buy two pair for $1.25 per pair. That was big bucks for me as I made only $0.35 per hour babysitting! Only so many people at a time were allowed into the store to buy nylons.

I remember how proud my Mom was when she got her W&D's charge card. It came in a brown leather card case. It had her name and address on it: Mrs. Jerry Richard.

In the store, they had a lady that would demonstrate coconut bon-bon candies. She would have the centers all prepared and dip them in melted coating. They were yellow, pink, green and white. She gave out samples. My friend and I would buy four of them in all different colors then split them in half and share them.

I also remember sound proof booths with turntables where you could take your choice of records to listen to. We'd both listen to seventy-eights for a good half-hour. Then we would each buy one record for seventy-nine cents each.

A neighbor lady went to work at W&D's, and I babysat her little girl for a few hours after school. I can remember how impressed everyone was that Betty had gotten a job at W&D's. She was to wear navy blue, black or brown skirts and sweaters that matched and white blouses. Many years later, Betty managed a small dress shop in Waynedale, which all came about because of her job at Wolf and Dessauer.

In the mid-1930s and 1940s, all brides wanted to start their married life with Fiesta dishes. The only place in Fort Wayne to get them was W&D. But of course, the best memories were of Santa, the big wreath and the animated window displays.

REMEMBERING W&D WITH DICK STONER

Dick Stoner has been a friend and mentor for thirty-five years. Sharing these memories with him was wonderful.

JK: What W&D events did you perform your magic show at over the years, Dick?

Dick: They had the Breakfast with Santa, *and they later telecast it. I did that a time or two. I also performed on the TV show a few times with*

Santa. I didn't perform on the train that went to Columbia City, but I did take my boys on it.

JK: What was the train ride like?

D: Phil Steigerwald used to walk up and down the aisle and talk with the kids. The kids felt like they were going to Chicago. It was so exciting for them, but it really only went to Columbia City.

JK: Did you work with Phil a lot over the years?

D: Oh yes. I worked a lot of Christmas shows where Phil would be the Santa for the event. For a number of years, I did a show at the country club, and he was always the Santa there. We also did a number of company parties where he would be Santa.

JK: You probably ran into him a lot at Christmastime then?

D: At the time he was the Santa, and I was the magician [laughs]! Most of the time, I would finish my kid's magic show and then bring Santa on. We'd sing "Jingle Bells" and then introduce Phil.

JK: What was Phil like at these events?

D: He was a great guy. A lot of times, he wouldn't be able to stay around long after the event to talk because he would do numerous appearances during the day, especially on those weekends. He would also bring his wife with him, sometimes as Mrs. Santa. In fact, I think my wife, Dee, sold her a Mrs. Claus outfit.

JK: The Santa outfits Phil always wore were top-notch weren't they?

D: Phil used to have a yak hair wig and beard. He was very proud of it because it was real hair, and of course, it was expensive. Later, they came out with the synthetic beards, but Phil stuck with the yak hair because he felt it was more authentic. That was his tradition.

JK: Did performing on Santa in WanDerland at Wolf and Dessauer give you the idea for the show you did on WANETV?

D: You mean Laurel and Hardy's Magic Castle? *Channel 15 was running Laurel and Hardy movies, and they wanted a host, so they contacted me. I had previously hosted* The Mickey Mouse Club.

JK: Fort Wayne had its own Mickey Mouse Club?

D: Yes, it was the local version. The host of the national show, Jimmy Dodd, came to town once, and we did some shows together at the embassy. We also did a tour of some of the Fort Wayne schools. We went to a school for kids with handicaps. I remember his manager saying that we had to hurry up because we had to get to some other schools. Jimmy still took his time with the kids.

I remember there was one little handicapped girl who told him, "I can type my name." She had a special typewriter. She would hit each key, and it took her a long time. The whole time, Jimmy's manager was going crazy telling him they had to get going, but that didn't matter to Jimmy. Finally, when the little girl had finished, Jimmy did the coolest thing. He said to her, "Can I keep that?" Can you imagine what that meant to that little girl? He had a knack like that for every little kid he came in contact with.

RECIPES

Since we all have fond memories of wonderful meals and treasured times spent over a dinner table with family and friends, we know that food is very strongly tied to our emotions. That's why certain smells wafting from the kitchen can inspire the return of childhood memories just as easily as paging through grandma's old photo album.

It's true that over the years, Wolf and Dessauer has been associated with some delicious meals that were served in the tearoom, as well as some wonderful pies and snacks served from their cafeteria. When you talk to people about Wolf and Dessauer, about 50 percent of the memories will revolve around food. But was it always like that?

The Wolf and Dessauer Tried and Proved OK Recipe Book, printed in 1914 by the Fort Wayne Printing Company, both amused and amazed us. Looking through the recipes made us wonder why you don't see dishes like "Fritter Beans," "Marrow Balls" or even "Prune Soup" anymore. Well, maybe that's because if we tried to serve these foods to children we'd have a horrible mutiny on our hands. And I wouldn't blame them.

Most of the recipes in this book sound like they were invented by Granny Clampet, and most deal with some kind of organ meat. We wondered, why they weren't "Tried and Proved *Delicious*"? Why were they just "OK"? Was it because they met the body's basic need for fuel and nobody died after eating them? All we know is that Martha Stewart never put out any cookbook with recipes that were proved "OK." So, for your enjoyment, here are some of those recipes. Maybe they will inspire you to run out to the kitchen to whip up a quick dinner!

Marrow Balls

4 tbs marrow
1 egg
salt
cayenne
nutmeg
soft bread crumbs

Cook marrow in frying pan. Strain. Beat egg. Add to marrow. Add seasonings and enough bread crumbs to make the right consistency to shape. Form into small balls and poach in hot water.

Author's note: Just wondering, how much trouble did these women go through to get all of this bone marrow? Why didn't they just use the meat on the bone? Would this be a good frugal recipe for today?

Bear

The haunch and saddle of a young bear is very good roasted, tasting almost like pork, but old bear meat is extremely hard and tough and is only palatable in a highly seasoned stew.

Author's note: Were there really bears in Fort Wayne in 1914 when this book was published? And furthermore, if there were, how many could they have killed and eaten to know that the old ones were only good for stew? Why didn't they just leave the old ones alone? If they tasted like pork, wouldn't it just be a lot safer to eat pigs and leave the bears alone? Bears can kill you.

Deviled Venison

Cut thick slices from rare-roasted venison, make slanting incisions and fill them with mixed mustard and salad oil. Brush slices with melted butter and dredge them with Gold Medal flour. Broil over coals until a good, deep brown and serve with butter.

Author's note: Were there deer roaming the streets of Fort Wayne, too? Wouldn't the bears have eaten them?

Recipes

Liver Dumplings

2 eggs
¼ cup butter
½ pound liver
1½ cups bread crumbs
chopped parsley
white herbs, salt and pepper
⅓ pound of fat bacon

Chop the liver and bacon (both raw) as fine as possible. Beat the eggs lightly and add the butter to them. Then add the meat, the seasonings and bread crumbs, adding more crumbs if necessary. This will depend on the softness or dryness of the crumbs and on the size of the eggs. The mixture should be just stiff enough to make a paste that can be formed into balls.

Divide into portions, roll smoothly in the hands and poach in boiling water for about 15 minutes.

Author's note: Liver. Enough said.

Broiled Sweetbreads

Parboil the sweetbreads and remove any membranes. Slice lengthwise, sprinkle with salt and pepper and place slices on hot broiler over a quick fire. Broil 5 minutes, turning once. Remove to a platter and serve with peas and toast.

Author's note: Well, maybe liver doesn't sound so bad!

Sweetbreads in Cases

two pairs of sweetbreads
1 can of mushrooms
1 cup of cream
½ cup of milk
1 tbs butter
½ tbs Gold Medal flour

¼ tsp salt
few grains cayenne

Parboil sweetbreads and remove membranes. Separate sweetbreads into small pieces. Trim mushrooms and cut each into four pieces. Melt butter. Add flour and seasoning. Cook together. Add scalded milk and cream, slowly. Cook together until smooth. To this, add the sweetbreads and mushrooms and cook 5 minutes. Serve in pastry shells.

NASTURTIUM SANDWICHES

Spread thin slices of white bread with mayonnaise. Use the petals of nasturtium flowers for filling, allowing some of the petals to come beyond the edge of the bread.

Author's note: Imagine coming home to this kind of sandwich after a hard day's work? How many of these would you have to eat to get full?

COFFEE JELLY

One half box of Knox Gelatin, soaked one hour in ½ cup cold coffee. Add 1 quart strong coffee and 1 cup sugar. Add 1 tsp vanilla. Cool in a crown mold, letting it stand on ice over night if possible. Turn onto a large platter and heap with whipped cream in the center as high as possible.

Author's note: Caffeine high?

This little recipe book proved to be such a treat to read. We would suggest that anyone interested get on the Internet and search eBay to try to get a copy for yourself. They are hard to come by, but there are still some out there. We've run across a couple from time to time. This fun book also had a section on "kitchen hints and helps" that we thought you'd enjoy. Some of them are medicinal in nature, so we must advise that these are intended only for fun. We don't know why anyone would want to, but don't try the following at home!

Recipes

A Help for a Sick Headache
A pinch of salt on the tongue, followed by a drink of water ten minutes afterward, often cures a sick headache.

Help for a Bruise
If sweet oil be applied to the skin after a blow or bruise, it will not turn black and blue.

For Gastric Trouble
To use olive oil daily is excellent for one having gastric trouble, and it will in some cases even prevent appendicitis.

For Gallstones
Olive oil is an excellent remedy in the case of gallstones; it reduces them to a soft substance and they pass the patient without pain. [Author's note: I've had gallstones. This won't work!]

For Digestion
An apple eaten before breakfast serves as a natural stimulant to the digestive organs. In fact, any fruit eaten raw is nutritious at breakfast.

Some Nutritional advice
Do Not Serve foods of like composition at the same meal, such as potatoes, rice and macaroni. They are all starch foods and do not give variety enough for the system. Food can often take the place of medicine. Eat variety at every meal thus giving the system all kinds of material to build on. [Author's note: Variety really is the key. Everyone should really have a little bit of bear meat, bone marrow or sweetbreads (but not all three!) in their diet every day.]

Ok, now let's get serious about recipes. At one point during our research, we did hear a rumor that the Courtside Café in downtown Fort Wayne is still serving some of the tearoom recipes. We can't confirm that, but it might be worth checking out. And now, we present you with some *proved really good* recipes!

Edith Goodyear's California Dream Bars

Edith Goodyear was the tearoom manager during its heyday.

First Layer
½ cup brown sugar
1 cup all-purpose flour
½ cup melted butter

Mix well. Line ungreased 7x11x1-inch cookie pan with flour mixture. Bake at 375 degrees for 10 minutes or until soft to the touch. Remove from oven and let stand. Turn off oven.

Second Layer
2 whole eggs
1 cup brown sugar
1 cup Angel Flake coconut
2 tbs all-purpose flour
¼ tsp salt
1 cup small pieces of pecans

Beat eggs until light-colored. Add the rest of the ingredients; blend well. Spread over baked first layer. Return to 350 degree oven. Bake 15 minutes. Cut when cool.

Pecan Cream Pie

This recipe was given to us by Marjorie Anderson of Columbia City for our newsletter.

1 oz. butter
⅜ cup 20 percent cream
1½ cups milk
¾ cup sugar
¼ tsp salt
¼ cup milk
3⅓ tbs cornstarch
2 egg yolks
¼ tsp vanilla
chopped, toasted pecans (1–2 cups, depending on taste preference)

Melt butter in top of double boiler. Add cream, 1½ cups of milk, sugar and salt. Stir until sugar is dissolved. Mix ¼ cup milk with cornstarch until smooth. Add beaten egg yolks. Pour small amount of sugar mixture into the cornstarch mixture and stir well. Stir and cook until thick. Remove from heat and add vanilla. Allow filling to cool.

Line bottom of 9-inch baked pie crust with chopped, toasted pecans. Add cooled filling. Top with whipped cream and sprinkle with toasted pecans.

W&D Frozen Salad

This one was provided to us by Marjorie Norton of Fort Wayne for our newsletter.

1 cup chopped nuts
1 two-pound can pineapple (crushed and drained)
1 small package marshmallows (colored are okay)
8 oz. Philadelphia cream cheese (softened)
1 pint whipping cream (whipped)
12 oz. Coolwhip (thawed)

Cream cheese and add pineapple and marshmallows. Add whipped cream. Fold in whipped cream or freeze.

Vinegar and Oil Salad Dressing

From Maxine Rudrow of Decatur.

Mix together the following and let stand overnight in the refrigerator:

1 pint salad oil
1 pint vinegar
3 cups of sugar
4 tbs salt
2 tbs white pepper
1 large grated onion
1 cup chopped peppers
1 cup chopped pimento

ICED LEMON SOUFFLÉ

1 envelope plain gelatin
2 tbs water
grated rind of four lemons
½ cup strained lemon juice
1 cup superfine sugar
1 cup egg whites (7–8), beaten very stiff
1 cup cream, whipped

Soften gelatin in water; add lemon rind, juice and sugar. Stir over low heat until gelatin is thoroughly dissolved; chill to syrup consistency.

Beat egg whites into mixture. Fold in whipped cream until thoroughly mixed. Tie a double band of waxed paper around the top of a 1-quart soufflé dish. Pour in the soufflé and chill.

When serving, remove waxed paper; decorate with additional whipped cream, paper-thin slices of lemon and fresh mint leaves.

TOMATO ASPIC

BASIC LEMON MIX
1 package of gelatin
⅓ cup of sugar
¼ cup lemon juice

1½ cups tomato juice
⅛ bay leaf
2 tbs chopped onion
¼ celery tops
2 tbs vinegar
pinch salt

Mix together basic lemon mix ingredients. Heat tomato juice with bay leaf, onion and celery tops. Strain over basic lemon mix. Add vinegar and salt. Yield: 6 molds.

Chicken Pie

2 cups chicken fat
4 cups flour
4¼ cup chicken broth
10 oz. chicken base
1 tbs egg shade color
10 oz. cooked chicken

Heat chicken fat. Blend in flour and stir until smooth. Add chicken base, egg shade color and chicken broth. Cook until thickened and no floury taste remains. Add cooked chicken meat. Pour into unbaked individual pie shells and top with unbaked pie crust. Bake in 350 degree oven about 45 minutes. Crimp edges and brush with cream

Escalloped Apples

Reprinted from the Fort Wayne News Sentinel.

3 pounds cooking apples, such as Macintosh or Jonathan
1 cup white sugar
½ cup flour
1 tsp cinnamon
½ tsp salt
2 tbs melted butter

Peel, core and cut apples in ¾-inch cubes. Place in buttered casserole dish about nine inches in diameter. Mix together the dry ingredients. Pour over the prepared apples and mix well. Pour melted butter over top. Cover and bake at 250 degrees for 45 minutes or until they just begin to cook. At this point, mix very gently with rubber spatula and bake remaining time, about 15 minutes, uncovered.

Tearoom Red Velvet Cake

1 cup vegetable shortening
2 eggs
1½ cups sugar

1 tsp cocoa powder
2 oz. red food coloring
2½ cups cake flour
1 tsp salt
1 cup buttermilk
1 tsp vanilla extract
1 tsp baking soda
1 tsp vinegar

FROSTING:
2 tablespoons flour
1 cup milk
1 cup unsalted butter
1 cup confectioners' sugar
1 teaspoon vanilla extract

Preheat oven to 350 degrees F. In the bowl of a mixer, cream together the shortening, eggs and sugar. In a small bowl, mix together cocoa and food coloring and add to the shortening mixture. Sift flour and salt together. Add to the batter alternately with the buttermilk in lumps of three. Add the vanilla extract. Fold in the baking soda and vinegar. Pour the batter into two greased 9-inch cake pans. Bake for 30 minutes or until a toothpick comes out clean. Let cool on a cooling rack and turn out the cakes from the pans.

Frosting: Over medium heat, cook the flour and milk until thickened. Let cool. In the bowl of an electric mixer, cream together the butter, sugar and vanilla until light and fluffy. Beat in the flour mixture. Frost the top of the first layer with frosting and set the second layer on top. Frost the entire cake with remaining frosting.

CHICKEN SALAD

2 tbs lemon juice
½ cup mayonnaise
1 tsp salt
3½ cups diced chicken
1 cup finely diced celery
⅓ cup slivered almonds

Combine lemon juice, mayonnaise and salt. Toss with chicken, celery and almonds. Blend well. Serve on bed of lettuce or your choice of bread.

SNICKERDOODLES

2 cups sugar, divided
1 cup Crisco® butter shortening OR 1 stick Crisco® butter shortening sticks
2 large eggs
2 tbs milk
1 tsp vanilla extract
2¾ cups Pillsbury BEST® all-purpose flour
2 tsp cream of tartar
1 tsp baking soda
¾ tsp salt
2 tsp ground cinnamon

Heat oven to 400 degrees. Combine 1½ cups sugar, shortening, eggs, milk and vanilla in bowl of electric mixer. Beat at medium speed until well blended. Combine flour, cream of tartar, baking soda and salt in medium bowl. Add gradually to shortening mixture at low speed. Mix just until blended.

Combine remaining ½ cup sugar and cinnamon in small bowl. Shape dough into 1-inch balls. Roll in sugar-cinnamon mixture. Place 2 inches apart on ungreased baking sheets. Bake 7 to 8 minutes. Cool 2 minutes on baking sheets. Place on cooling racks to cool completely.

Appendix

RANDOM WOLF AND DESSAUER FACTS

Wolf and Dessauer had the first escalator in the city.

In 1938, sparing no expense for the good of its patrons, Wolf and Dessauer was the first major store to install air conditioning.

At one time, Wolf and Dessauer had the second-largest American flag in the nation draped across the front of its building.

W&D was the only store of its kind in Fort Wayne to have a three-piece orchestra playing in the cafeteria at noon for the enjoyment of its dining customers.

W&D sold $3 million in war bonds at the Washington and Calhoun corner window. It was the largest sale of war bonds in the area.

Wolf and Dessauer gave out green stamps with purchases.

Inside the store, the company hired gloved and uniformed operators to run all of the elevators.

Wolf and Dessauer introduced the first Paris fashions to Fort Wayne beginning in 1926. The fashions were flown in by zeppelin.

In 1941, Wolf and Dessauer banned the sale of all products made in "belligerent countries" to help inspire patriotism in the community.

Did you know that during World War II, Fort Wayne newspapers sponsored the famed American pilot Charles Lindbergh on a trip to Fort Wayne? Because Lindbergh was believed to be a Nazi sympathizer, Mr. G. Irving Latz urged the paper to cancel the trip. The newspaper refused his request, so Mr. Latz withdrew all Wolf and Dessauer advertising from the Fort Wayne papers for the next two years.

Because of the enduring patriotic spirit of Wolf and Dessauer, it found itself the recipient of a $^1/_5$-scale replica of the Liberty Bell in the summer of 1968. It was made by a four-hundred-year-old firm called Whitechapel Bell Foundry in London, England. The bell stood thirteen inches high, was mounted on an oak base and was meant to be rung. Wolf and Dessauer displayed the bell "to commemorate the faith of Americans in the enduring principles of freedom for all."

We all know that Ayers eventually bought and took over all that we remember of Wolf and Dessauer. Do you know, though, that before the buyout by L.S. Ayers, the stores in Huntington and Fort Wayne were sold to City Stores in 1966. When City Stores bought W&D, the new owners promised that they would not have any changes in personnel, management or operating policies. They made good on their promise until the sale to Ayers took place in December 1969 for an undisclosed sum.

Although Lutheran Hospital in Fort Wayne has a treehouse in its lobby, it wasn't the first to do so. The Junior Boys Department at the South Town Mall store had a wooden treehouse overlooking the whole department for the boys to play in while their mothers shopped.

In 1946, famous bandleader Xavier Cugat visited the record department of Wolf and Dessauer.

Almost from the store's inception, the owners took special care of their employees and the families of those employees. The annual Children's Christmas Party was an event sponsored by Wolf and Dessauer management and one that became more grand and festive every year. The party was held in the beginning of December, and children as well as grandchildren of employees were all welcome. There were often more than six hundred children in attendance to join in the fun of candy, cookies, magic, movies, puppets and baton twirlers. Of course, the crowning moment was the arrival of Santa and Wee Willie WanD, who passed out presents and listened to the long wish lists of the little ones.

In 1946, W&D celebrated the store's fiftieth anniversary with an event unsurpassed in Fort Wayne musical history. In commemoration, W&D presented the Philharmonic orchestra and chorus with four soloists from the Metropolitan Opera, singing Verdi's *Messa da Requiem*. Almost five thousand people attended these performances, and twenty-four thousand invitational cards were clipped to the commemorative Philharmonic programs and mailed, inviting W&D's charge-holding customers to be their listening guests through the medium of a special radio broadcast.

CONCLUSION

Anyone who has ever watched a science fiction movie has seen at least one involving some sort of time machine. There is something fascinating about the possibility of traveling back in time to relive a sweet memory or perhaps even altering it in order to affect a present-day event. For us, writing about Wolf and Dessauer has been like a time machine in that it transported us back to a kinder, gentler time when people lived in the moment, without the distraction and noise that seem to permeate our lives today.

To see what I mean, walk into any restaurant and just observe. You'll see entire families sitting together but totally ignoring one another. Dad's on his cellphone talking to a business client. Mom is on her phone Facebooking, and the kids are in constant contact with the same people they just spent their entire school day with. The weirdest thing about that is that the kids do all of their talking via texting. They don't even bother to speak anymore!

Perhaps you've heard of the high tech/high touch theory. It basically suggests that the more technically advanced a society becomes, the more we long for meaningful human interaction. On that note, it's no surprise that behind almost every Wolf and Dessauer story someone has related to us, there is a basic picture of one person relating to another in a way that was deeply personal and caring.

It would be difficult to recall how many times we've heard, "Someone should buy one of those buildings downtown and bring that store back!" I think what they are really saying is, "I wish we could go back to a time when people smiled, asked if there was something they could help you with and actually meant it!"

Sad to say, no one will ever be able to bring Wolf and Dessauer back, but hopefully this book has been, and will continue to be, your personal time machine—one that you can use anytime you feel the need to remember.

ABOUT THE AUTHORS

Jim and Kathie Barron are the authors of three other books on the subject of Fort Wayne history. Jim is a thirty-five-year radio broadcast veteran and is part of the award-winning morning team on WBCL radio in Fort Wayne. He has also been a professional comedian and a magician/illusionist for more than forty years and performs frequently for church, fundraising and festival events. Kathie is a writer and singer and is planning a future book on Robison Park, an amusement park that was a big part of Allen County history. Jim and Kathie are the parents of four children and four grandchildren and thank Jesus Christ for all the blessings in their lives.

Visit us at
www.historypress.net

www.ingramcontent.com/pod-product-compliance
Lightning Source LLC
Chambersburg PA
CBHW060805100426
42813CB00004B/952